Maria Rosaria Belgiorno & Alessandro Lentini †

Cyprus in the Prehistory of Wine

Archaeology, Legends and Archaeometry on a symbol of god

with a preface by Gherardo La Francesca

Edited by M.R Belgiorno

Gherardo La Francesca: Preface.

Maria Rosaria Belgiorno: Introduction

Amber Roy: proofreading and short review

Antonio De Strobel:
Computer processing of all illustrations
© Photographs and elaborations:
pages iii, iv, xiii, 1, 3, 7, 16, 18, 23,
24, 25, 26, 28, 29, 31 Fig. 19, 33,
37, 39, 41, 43, 44, 45, 46, 51 Fig. 37,
57, 74, 78, 82, 84, 87, 88; hard cover.

Edited by Maria Rosaria Belgiorno
Associazione Culturale Armonia

Copyright © 2017 Maria Rosaria Belgiorno

All rights reserved.

ISBN: 978 889 0574108

to Alessandro

(memory by Lavinia De Strobel)

Scented soap of Aleppo
as old as the oil and laurel leaves,
smiles lost under the warm sun of Cyprus
on the excavation, between earth and carob trees.

Strange slides left on the walls,
collections of pollens and
mysterious enchantments under the microscope
took place between your hands of professor.

The smiles of nocturnal jokes
brightened up the mood of us
not sleeping, but playing with you
while Morpheus held you in his arms.

As the rain comes down clear
and blesses the Earth from clouds
so, my thoughts today
may rise up
to tell you goodbye
A hug
Lavinia.

(memory by Sara Elifani)

I had the pleasure to know and to work with Alessandro for few years, on and off, in Cyprus, on site and in Rome, in his turf: the laboratory. Alessandro is a great person and friend! He is ironic and funny, with his quirkiness and roman accent that made me laugh and at the same time left me puzzled trying to understand him.

He has a joke ready all the time, it is impossible not to be happy and light hearted around him! He really is great in uplifting your spirit!

He is also an unstoppable worker, I've learned a lot from him, I just wish I spent more time with him...I sometimes actually wonder where would I be now if I did that...

I just wanna conclude saying Alessandro is funny, is quirky and a really good person! And I am sure he's generating lots of laughs and puzzled face wherever he is! No matter where you are, you'll always be here with all of us forever!

With love.

Sara

CONTENTS

List of Figures — ii

Preface — xi
Gherardo La Francesca

Introduction — 1
Maria Rosaria Belgiorno

Archaeology and Legends — 5
Maria Rosaria Belgiorno

Archaeometry — 57
Alessandro Lentini

LIST OF FIGURES

Archaeology and legend:

Fig. 1: Fossil leaf of *ampelidea* 50 million of years, from the *"pesciaia"* of Bolca, Museo dei Fossili di Bolca, Vestenanova, Verona — 5
Fig. 2: The route of *Vitis silvestris* to the Mediterranean — 7
Fig. 3: Vitis spread in the Fertile Crescent, Jordan Valley, and Egypt. — 9
Fig. 4: Pits for wine making in the Cave of Birds of Novarank, Areni, (Armenia). — 10
Fig. 5: Italy. Map of archaeological sites with presence of grape seeds. — 11
Fig. 6: King Scorpion Mace-Head, Temple of Horus, Hierakonpolis, 1908. E3632, Ashmolean Museum, Oxford. — 12
Fig. 7: Hajji Firuz (Armenia) the biconical vase analysed by P. Mc Govern. — 15
Fig. 8: Wineskin hung in an old house in Cyprus. — 16
Fig. 9: Comparison between jars of Hajji Firuz, Godin Tepe, Egypt and Erimi. — 17
Fig.10: Geographical position of Erimi along the Kouris River. — 19
Fig.11: Erimi excavation of a Neolithic house in 1932. — 20
Fig.12: Dikaios excavations at Erimi: — 21
Fig.13: Wine jar from the Neolithic village of Erimi. — 22
Fig.14: Traditional "pithari" of XVIII and XIX centuries. — 23
Fig.15: Documentation of the analyses in the laboratory of Nicosia Archaeological Museum. — 24
Fig.16: Analysis and results under the UV Lamp of a sample. — 25
Fig.17: Analysis results of askos (T.97 n. 277) from Souskiou. — 26
Fig.18: Human head askos (Souskiou?), S. Barnaba Monastery Museum, Northern Cyprus. — 27
Fig.19: Myc. B Tablet with "di-wo-nu-so" 1400BC, Chania Archaeological Museum, Crete. — 28
Fig.20: Cypriot stamp with a 7000BC Stone bowl

Fig.20: (horned handle) from Kalavassos/Tenta. - 29
Fig.21: Palaeolithic Venus from Laussel
20.000 BC, Musée d'Aquitaine, Bordeaux France. - 30
Fig.22: Analysis of a clay horn from Vounous T.164 n°61. - 31
Fig.23: Grape pressing model 2000/1-25,
Archaeological Museum Nicosia. - 32
Fig.24: Protodynastic pressing model from Abydos,
Cairo Museum. - 33
Fig.25: Cypriot Chalcolithic wine jar from
the antiquary market, private collection. - 33
Fig.26: Double neck scenic jug from Pyrgos, with
grape pressing. Archaeological Museum Limassol. - 34
Fig.27: Model from a Predynastic tomb of Naqada,
Cairo Museum. - 35
Fig.28: Shrine Models from Kochati,
Archaeological Museum Nicosia. - 36
Fig.29: *Sgraffito* ware wedding dish with drinking
horn and wine jug. Ashmolean Museum Oxford. - 36
Fig.30: Linos in the Aghios Georghios' cave, Erimi. - 38
Fig.31: Wine Proto krater, Pyrgos/Mavroraki n°. 466,
Limassol Museum. - 39
Fig.32: Wine storage jar from Pyrgos/Mavroraki,
n. 355 Limassol Museum. - 40
Fig.33: Jug with bucrania and snakes from
Pyrgos/Mavroraki n. 423, Limassol Museum. - 41
Fig.34: Jug with human figure and snakes,
Pyrgos/Mavroraki n. 107, Limassol Museum. - 42
Fig.35: Cyprus Early Bronze Age Tulip- bowl from Vounous
T.91 n.14, Fitzwilliam Museum, Cambridge. - 44
Fig.36: Minoan gem: Corpus of Minoan and Mycenaean Seals,
volume: IX no. 9, Paris *Cabinet des medailles*:
MM I; CMS-IX-009- 1. - 44
Fig.37: Cyprus, Kato Paphos, House of Dionysos: III AD
Mosaic with the arrive of Ikarios and the villagers drunk. - 46
Fig.38: Aghia Triada model of girl on swing:
Iraklion Museum Crete. - 46

Archaeometry

Fig.1: Wild Euro-Asiatic grape distribution between
Mediterranean and Persian Gulf - 56
Fig.2: Archaeological Mediterranean sites with macro
remains of Vitis sp. - 59
Fig.3: Grape seed from SU PY05/GH9L4.
Morphology roundish to heart-shaped. - 64
Fig.4: Grape seeds from SU PY06L5/2. Morphology
oval to pear-shaped, with distinct elongated tip. - 64
Fig.5: Grape seeds from SU PY04F8L1 Morphology
intermediate between that of seeds of wild and
cultivated grapes. - 65
Fig.6: SUs G9L3, G9L4, G9l7, carbonized seeds of
different type of *Vitis* ssp. – Image processing
colour threshold for the biometric measurements. - 65
Fig.7: First group of *vitis* seeds from Pyrgos/Mavroraki
typical of cultivated grapes. - 67
Fig.8: Second group of vitis seeds from Pyrgos/Mavroraki;
intermediate range between wild and cultivated grapes - 67
Fig.9: Fragment of askos from US Py04 G8 n°13: the green
coloration of the solution reveals that it contains high
rate of tartaric acid, typical of the wine produced in the
Mediterranean area. - 69
Fig.10: Wine jug US Py05 I 7 n. 238; analysis results. - 69
Fig.11: Analyses result on a fragment of jar from the
excavation of P. Dikaios at Erimi 1933, n°127 ex 2. - 73
Fig.12: Chemical structure of tartaric acid, generally in nature,
is found like Dextro-rotary stereoisomer (if illuminated with
polarized light rotates towards the right). During the
fossilization, it is transformed in a racemic acid. - 73
Fig.13: Pyrgos, Stratigraphic Units PY J4, levels -180 >-230 cm,
pollens of *Pistacia*. - 74
Fig.14: Lentini taking samples for the palynological stratigraphy. - 76
Fig.15: Kyrenia mountain range about 100 km long and rising to
over 1000 meters runs parallel to the coastline and forms a
sort of natural barrier between the coast and the interior. - 78

Fig.16: Populus, Alnus and Salix along a stream. - 81
Fig.17: Cultivation of *Vitis vinifera* L. ssp. *sativa* HEGI by the "little tree" method at an altitude of 900-1000 meters (Troodos mountains). - 82
Fig.18: Rain Distribution in Cyprus. - 87

PREFACE

Gherardo La Francesca

"Thank you very much for your letter concerning the archaeological discoveries made by the Italian National Research Council (CNR)".

Thus, began a two-page document that the President of the Republic of Cyprus, Tassos Papadopoulos addressed to me in June 2005, when I was Ambassador of Italy in Nicosia.

The letter, as the President said, was signed by himself, focused on the relevance of the discovery of the oldest wine in the Mediterranean, traces of which were found in jars unearthed in the '30s, in the chalcolithic Erimi village near Limassol. Then it continued in congratulations for the excellent work done by the Italian team of CNR ITABC-coordinated by Maria Rosaria Belgiorno, and in appreciation for the great importance that the news concerning the discovery had obtained in the international media.

He then expressed the gratitude of the Cypriot government and its consequent willingness to "... provide every possible help and encouragement for the continuation of fruitful cooperation".

I have kept with pleasure this document, eloquent proof of the importance that culture can play as diplomatic action instrument, with potential political repercussions.

The story had begun a few months before, in my office at the Embassy in Nicosia. With Maria Rosaria Belgiorno, we were taking stock of the progress of excavations carried out by CNR ITABC at Pyrgos and future prospects in the archaeological sector.

Almost randomly, the talk fell on the wine, and some jars of the late Neolithic whose shape, like that of Roman amphorae, gave grounds for suspecting that it had been used to contain wine.

"If we can prove it - said dr. Belgiorno - we would have evidence that, as early as so remote, Cyprus knew the winemaking process and the need to store wine in jars with a conical base that would collect the wine dregs.

This would be an important finding given that, to date, no one has scientifically proven that this process was known and applied in this area. In other words, we would have discovered one of the oldest wines of the Mediterranean".

The prospect seemed immediately attractive. I thought it would be a fascinating adventure, which would have earned us respect and gratitude from our Cypriot friends. Then, I asked how we could proceed, what or who could help us perform the necessary analysis.

The answer was a name: Alessandro Lentini chemical and Archeometrician at the ITABC- CNR.

He would be able to do the analysis and provide concrete evidence about what was only a hypothesis at the time. Luckily, it was not difficult, in the low season, finding a flight return to Rome Larnaca at affordable costs and, as to the hospitality Cyprus was spoiled for choice.

Within a couple of weeks, I met Lentini, and I immediately had the feeling of being in front of a person who met two precious gifts: a great professional competence and a real passion for his work.

Then began the search for all Cyprus an ultraviolet lamp with a given frequency of nanometres. It was certainly not the kind used for out-of-season tans; it was, soon discovered it was identical to that used in dentists' offices to sterilize the instruments.

To retrieve the lamp, we asked hospitality at the Department of Antiquities of Cyprus who made available the restoration laboratories at the National Museum of Nicosia and Limassol District Museum.

Gherardo La Francesca armed with tripod and camera
in the laboratory of Nicosia Muuseum.

Lentini took samples of material scraped from the walls and inside of the vessels, and dissolved it in sulphuric acid and other chemicals in glass ampoules.

After a few minutes, the mixture moved to white porcelain trays and was placed under the ultraviolet lamp. Armed with tripod and camera, a privileged witness of this little magic, I saw that the concoction was taking a nice green colour.

This happened, as I had anticipated, only due to the presence of tartaric acid released from the wine storage. We have proven that the vessels had contained wine and that those jars found at Erimi in the 30's excavation of had been used to preserve one of the oldest wines in the Mediterranean, perhaps the oldest.

We decided to include in the month of Italian culture that, the Embassy was arranging for the month of June, a small exhibition devoted to wine, would occur, in collaboration with the Department of the Antiquities, which declared itself available to the event. Before the opening, we decided to make the announcement to the media by organizing a small press conference at the Embassy.

In truth, it was much less small than imagined. Present were all Cypriot warheads, but also the Ansa, the CNA and Reuter. The next day, the agencies around the world, from Finland to 'Argentina and Korea gave the announcement of the discovery.

The President of the Republic of Cyprus took pen and paper to express his thanks.

Sometimes even results of high political profile can easily be achieved on condition that they can count on competent and passionate people like only researchers can be.

INTRODUCTION

Maria Rosaria Belgiorno

This book tells the story of an investigation in which merged together the different expertise of two colleagues who have worked side by side for 15 years, in the same institution the ITABC-CNR.

Alessandro Lentini died suddenly of a heart attack the 10th march 2016 returning from one of the Congresses of Archaeometry, which he always participated with enthusiasm. This is one of the papers we were working and I am happy that it appears after one year of his passing. But this will not be his last publication.

Far to claim to be exhaustive about the most ancient Mediterranean wine or of the Cypriot wine, *"Cyprus in the prehistory of wine"* is a report of the search path carried out to find an answer to our curiosity.

It tells something regarding the Cypriot wine in prehistory, not going over the Late Bronze age. On our route, we found the collaboration of many people and institutions.

It has been the occasion to taste the scholarly and friendly collaboration of the Department of the Antiquities of Cyprus direction and archaeological staff, opening the doors of the storage rooms and laboratories of Nicosia and Limassol museums and involving themselves in the research.

A. Lentini and M. R. Belgiorno in the laboratory of Limassol Museum

The Italian Embassy in Nicosia adopted immediately the subject, supporting financially, and helping in finding the necessary equipment to carry out the investigation. They also aided the organisation of an exhibition on the Cypriot wine for the 2005 Italian Culture month: "Cyprus 6000 years of wine Culture", Nicosia Archaeological Museum 30June- 30July.

The event was arranged with the passionate collaboration of Sara Elifani, Laura Paterlini and Laura D'Isep (future archaeologists), who were in Cyprus for a stage at the excavation at Pyrgos/Mavroraki.

The Italian Embassy published in 2005 a booklet for the event, including a catalogue of the most interesting vases and a short report of our investigation, which is the starting point of this book, and has the same title *"Cyprus in the Prehistory of wine"*. This enabled us to add what was omitted at the time lack of space.

The search path made to enter the topic has made known to us unknown aspects of ancient Cypriot agricultural tradition, jealously preserved in the villages of the Troodos, where you can find the results of a wine culture seems to arise from the very heart of the island lost in a past whose history has not yet been defined with absolute certainty. Indeed, most of the names of the famous vineyards of Cyprus do not correspond today to any cultivation of grapes.

Even the famous *Commandaria* the medieval "Quillac", which took the name from the village of Kellaki is today produced far from its original land.

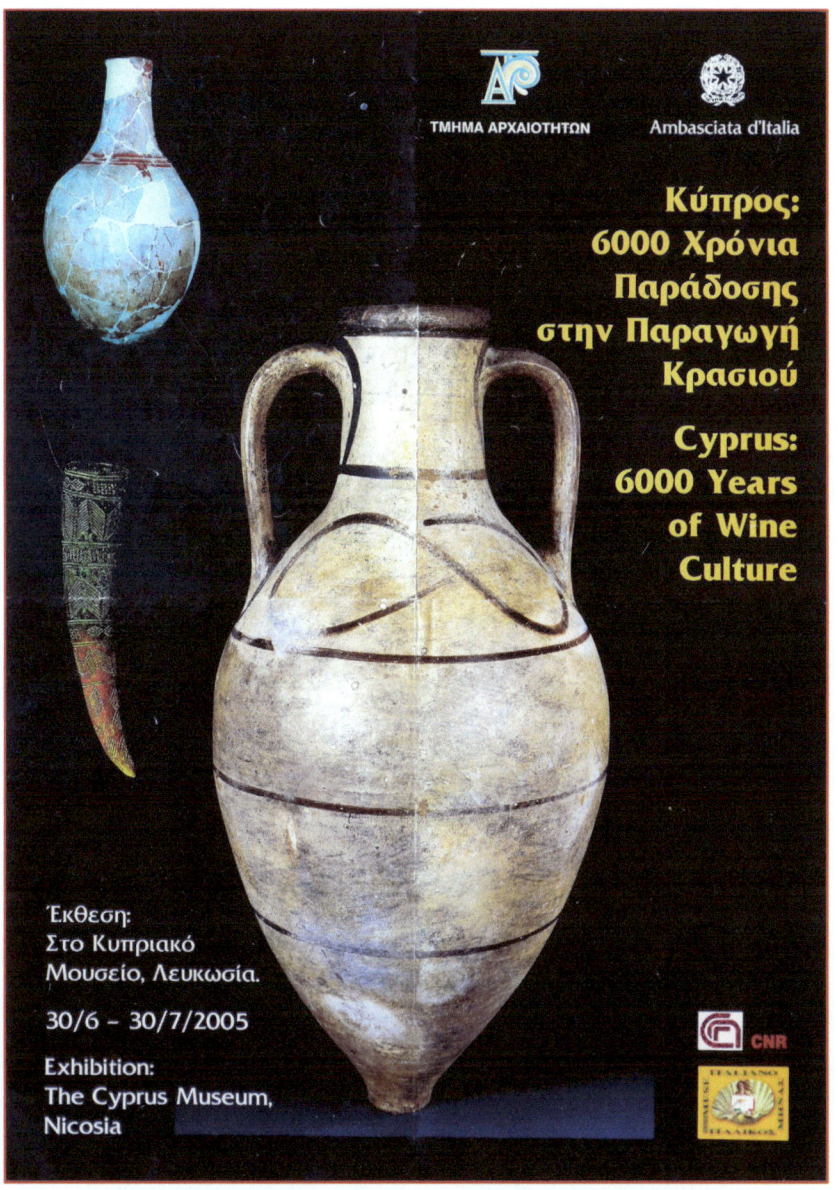

Poster of the exhibition Cyprus 6000 years of wine Culture

New names are gradually replacing the historical names of the celebrated wines of Cyprus mentioned in the Homeric poems.

But the old tradition of Cyprus, which used more wine than beer, preserving like a treasure the precious liquid in large jars hidden under the floor of the houses, still survives in its family and culinary use.

For centuries wine and olive oil have been the main ingredients in pharmaceutical herbs coming from the endemic Flora of the island, according to old preparations, based mainly on resins, gums, bulbs, and recipes surviving through the oral tradition.

Some of them probably were still known in the Bronze age as the results of the Archaeometry investigation made on the archaeological material from Pyrgos/Mavroraki suggest.

In antiquity wine was used for many purposes and employed even for cosmetics and magical potions, to preserve food and meat, to cure skin and disinfect wounds. It was the main ingredient in the joyful and sad celebrations, and in religious ceremonies. In its processing and preserving, human ingenuity has perhaps created the first forms, industrial ceramics, but also the most fascinating and complex forms of drinking.

In this regard, we can consider Cyprus a country that has given the best of herself starting with the Erimi jars of the Chalcolithic period.

ARCHAEOLOGY AND LEGENDS

Maria Rosaria Belgiorno

Speaking of wine and its importance in history, it deals with a very broad subject, covering cultural, religious and economies, which have left indelible imprints in human society. Wine is something sacred, the only product authorized to represent God, the blood of Christ. Centuries of wisdom firmly establish its importance and superiority over any other agricultural product.

To note how wine took the position of one of the most important agricultural products of the antiquity, largely employed in the preparation of pharmaceutical remedies, we must go over a brief history of the oldest wine and its relationship with the human society.

In 1875, John Murray published the entry "Vinum" (12011208) in his Dictionary of Greek and Roman antiquities, saying *Vitis vinifera* came from the Himalayas and the TransCaucasian region. Subsequently, in 1929 the Russian scholar M.G. Popov confirmed his thesis[1]. Today,

---

* Fossilized *vitis* leaf of the Pleistocene
[1]M.G. Popov 1929: Dikie plodovye dereb'ja i kustarniki Srednej Azii.Trud. Po prikl, in *Botanike*, XXII, 3. 241-483; N. Vavilov 1930. Wild Progenitors

most researchers agree that the wild grape *Vitis vinifera silvestris* was originally from that region. However, Paleo-grape ancestors existed 60 million years ago, even in Italy[2].

As early as 1800, it was known that the natural environment of the grape was the mountain, and it was generally accepted that the first wild grape was cultivated for the first time in the Himalayan valleys.

Moreover, the scholars considered possible that the distribution of the cultivated grape had followed the same path of the natural spread of wild grapes. This advises that both species of *Vitis silvestris* and *Vitis sativa* (IE cultivated) circulated according to precise geographic ranges and, passing over the mountains and valleys, it arrived in the Mediterranean finding there the best habitat to reproduce.

More recently a search of FAO on the grapevine genome, conducted simultaneously in different universities and research centres, has revealed that domestication of the *wild vines* took place in the South Caucasus between the Caspian and the Black Sea [3](Fig.2).

The contribution of genetic Mediterranean variants of *Vitis silvestris* in *Vitis vinifera* (sativa) remains a problem yet to be solved since it seems that the *sativa* has additional genes that might come from the wild endemic species

---

of the Fruit Trees of the Turkistan and the Caucasus and the Problem of the Origin of the Fruit Trees, IX *International Horticulture Congress London*, 271-286.

[2] C. D'Ancona 1881: Gli antenati della vite vinifera, in *Atti della Regia Accademia dei Georgofili*, XIII; E. Schiemann 1953.Vitis in Neolithicum der Mark Brandenburg, in *Züchter*, XXIII, 1-11, 318-327; A. Stummer 1911. Zur Urgeschichte der Reben und des Weinbaues, in Mitteilungen der Anthropologischen Gesellschaft in *Wien, 61*, 238296.

[3] 3 S. Myles, A.R. Boyko, C.L. Owens, P.J. Brown, F. Grassi, M.K. Aradhya, B. Prins, B. Reynolds, A. Chiah, J.M. Wareh, D. Bustamante and E.S. Buckler 2011. *Genetic structure and domestication history of the grape*, Agricultural Sciences, Washington University 1, 6; Proceedings of the National Academy of Sciences.

Fig.2: The route of *Vitis silvestris* to arrive in the Mediterranean.

Considering that wine can be made from both species *silvestris* and *sativa*, and the grapes can grow at different latitudes forcing their adaptation, it is obvious that the best quality developed in the habitat chosen by the plant itself.

Professor Pisani, one of the most important Italian scholars on the wine, who wrote hundreds of books on the topic, confirmed, that wine is one of the first discoveries of man and was probably made in rock pits many centuries before the invention of pottery.

This happened somewhere along the so-called wine belt and most probably in different places almost simultaneously.

Therefore, we never know who invented wine.

Archaeological data suggests that later the cultivation spread in the western area of the Fertile Crescent, in the Jordan Valley, and in Egypt. Hence, the cultivation and winemaking knowledge spread to the West and Central Europe (Fig.3).

Archaeometry investigations of different species of ancient grapevine have shown that in all ages, both wild and cultivated grapes have been used to produce wine, often mixing the different qualities[4].

We can recognize the *Vitis silvestris* from the *Vitis sativa* by the shape of the seeds, but we cannot use the presence of the seeds as a diagnostic or chronological index of the wine knowledge, as the *Vitis silvestris* is still widespread and used as a rootstock.

Invisible spies of the grape presence are also the pollens, which can be identified by experts in the stratigraphy of a digging, but it is difficult to say if they belong to the wild or cultivated grapevine.

However, the study of Palaeobotany allows us, through the examination of pollens, to identify variants and transverse grafts selected by man to produce fine wines.

---

[4] P.E. Mc Govern, J.S. Fleming and S.H. Katz 1995. *The Origins and Ancient History of Wine*, NewYork and Luxembourg.

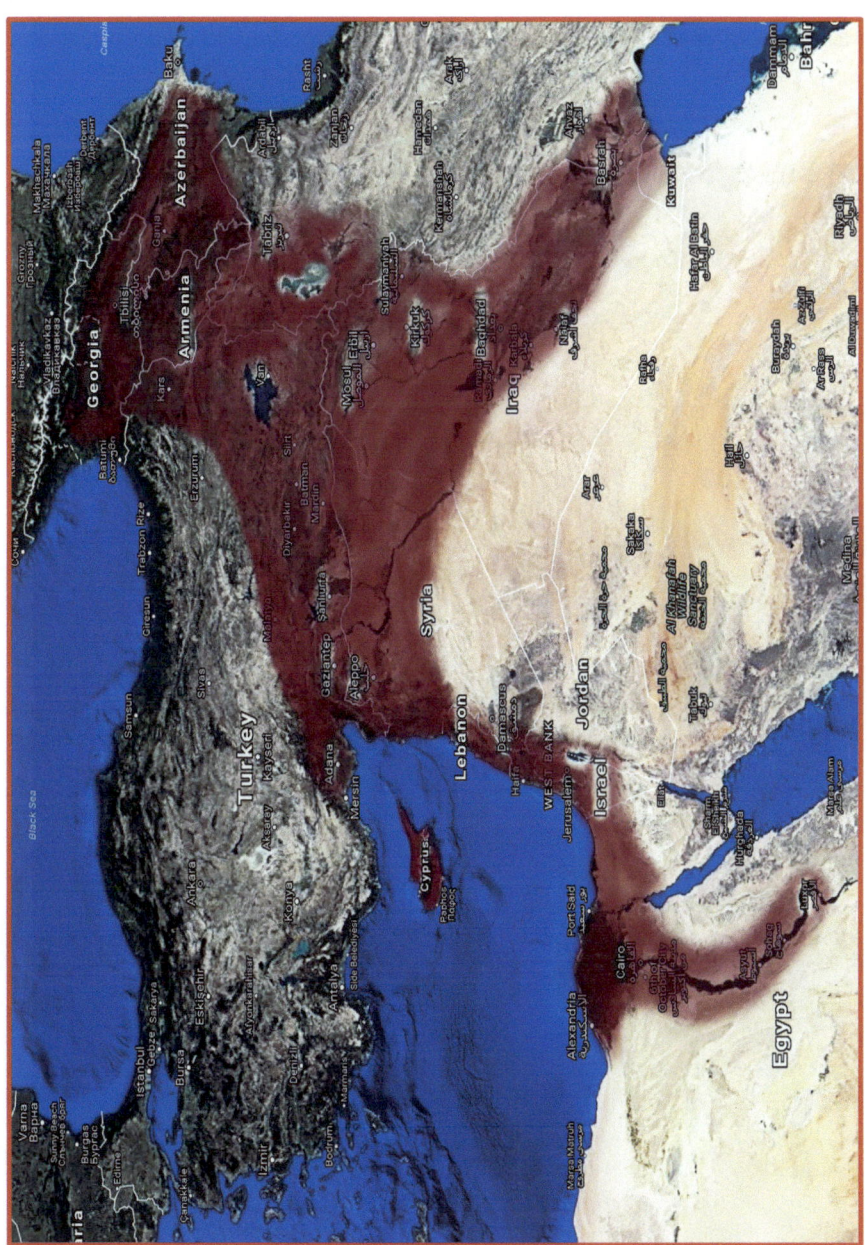

Fig.3: Spread in the Fertile Crescent, Jordan Valley and Egypt.

We do not know what the rating index was, if it was considered the best wine with the higher alcohol content or the most aromatic one. Today we know that the oldest grapes employed to produce wine, dating from the 5th millennium BC were founded in Armenia in the Cave of Birds (*Trchuneri*) of Noravank, in the Vayoz Zor' Valley, near the village of Areni in Armenia[5] (Fig.4).

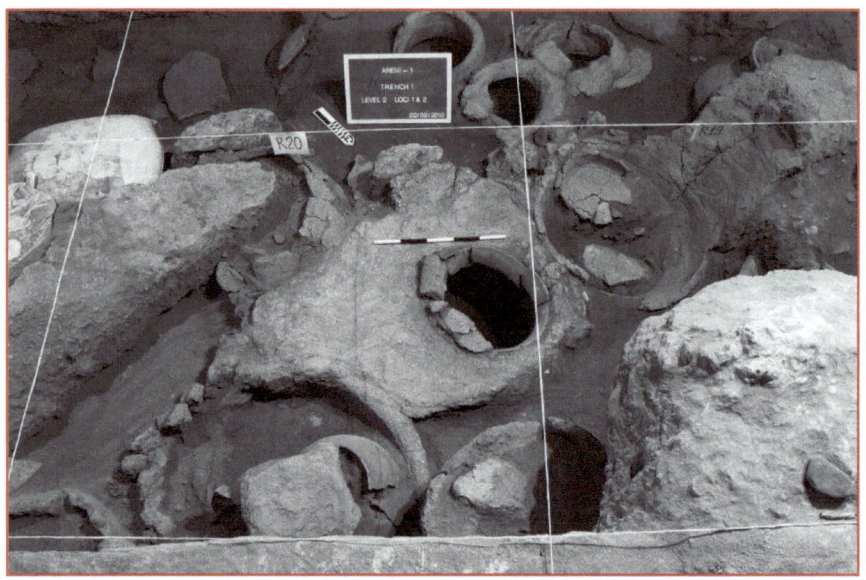

Fig.4: Pits for wine making in the Cave of Birds of Novarank.

---

[5] The Cave of Birds of Noravank, at Areni (Armenia) has a special climate. It was used as warehouse for agricultural commodities since the end of the Neolithic. Among the organic finds recovered of the Chalcolithic period, (C14 dated), there is a mummified goat, a leather shoe, some wood and bone tools, dried seeds and fruits, as well as crystal remains of grape processing in earthenware jars cut into the rock itself. National Geographic Magazine, January 2011; H. Barnard, A.N. Dooley, G. Areshian, B. Gasparyan, and K.F. Faull 2011. Chemical Evidence for Wine Production Around 4000 BCE in the Late Chalcolithic Near Eastern Highlands, in *Journal of Archaeological Science* 38: 977–984.
- K.N. Wilkinson, B. Gasparian, R. Pinhasi, P. Avetisyan, R. Hovsepyan, D. Zardaryan, G.E. Areshian, G. Bar-Oz and A. Smith 2012. Areni-1 Cave, Armenia: A Chalcolithic–Early Bronze Age settlement and ritual site in the southern Caucasus, in *Journal of Field Archaeology* vol. 37 N°1, 20-33.

Before this discovery in 2010, the presence of grape seeds in many archaeological contexts had caused assumptions about the Neolithic production of wine even in Italy.

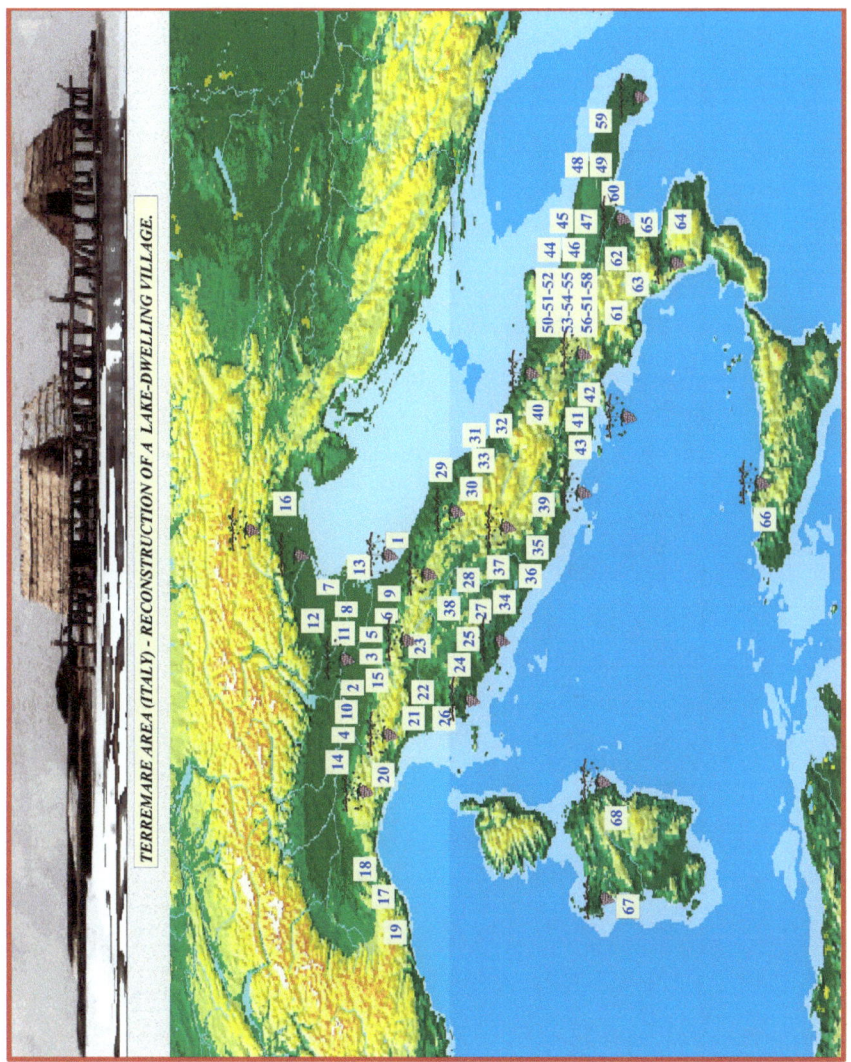

Fig.5: Italy. Map of archaeological sites with presence of grape seeds.

However, if we had to consider the findings of seeds in archaeological contexts, Italy would not only be one of the oldest places where wine was produced, but also a country involved in the traffic of wine from the fifth millennium BC (Fig.5).

Furthermore, the very name of wine may go back to a much older age. In fact, the word "v)ino, wine" seems to derive from two Egyptian hieroglyphics "wnsy" that identifies grapes and "smw" that identifies the wine press. Even though the wine in ancient Egypt was called "*irp*". Both words "wnsy" and "smw" appear in proto dynastic records from the tombs of Abydos (3200 BC). Nevertheless, it is curious to note that the word (*irp, winum* dating back to the 2nd Dynasty) anticipates the word grapes (wnsy), as if the Egyptians had known wine before the plant that produces it. This chronological interchange seems to find an explanation of the discovery of the 700 wine-jars found in the grave of King Scorpion in 1990 (Fig.6).

Fig.6: King Scorpion Mace Head, Temple Horus Hierakonpolis, AN1896-1908. E3632, Ashmolean Museum, Oxford

The tomb was built around 3150 BC (Naqada III A2 period) and the vessels containing spiced wine were from different sites of Southern Palestine. Analyses carried out on the clay of the stoppers that sealed the jars indicated they were Egyptian. This observation opened several discussions on the taste, use and adding of spices, according to the ancient herbal medicine of Egypt, before joining the funeral equipment of King Scorpion[6].

Seeds of grapes were still found in Predynastic (4000-3050 BC) settlements of Tell El-Farain (Buto) and Tell IbrahimAwad, located in the Nile Delta.[7]

From the tomb of King Djoser (III dynasty, Old Kingdom around 2600 BC), we have the first written document that affirms the king's wine came from "the vineyard of the red house of the king's house in the town of *Senpu* in the western *nomes*". Based on the evidence it seems that in Egypt the history of wine follows in parallel to that of pharmaceutical compounds and cosmetics[8].

The distinction that the Egyptians had among the different types of wine, identifying notes through the smell and taste, makes us realize how much they were experts in recognizing the compositions of fragrances. Moreover, the common factor in between wine and the scent lies above all in the terms used to describe the fragrance.

Distinguishing the base notes, heart, and head, associating them with flowers, fruits, plants, soil, and minerals, as well as attributes such as sweet, sour, pungent, warm, full-bodied and enveloping.

The categories of aromas through which wine is described are substantially three: primary or varietal aromas, secondary aging factors perfumes and tertiary, the aromas from fermentation. The same categories by which the scents were described before use of alcohol and chemical aromas.

---

[6] B. Handwerk 2009. Scorpion King's Wines Egypt's Oldest, Spiked with Meds, in *National Geographic News* April 13. McGovern, Patrick E., Ulrich Hartung, Virginia R. Badler, Donald L. Glusker, and Lawrence J. Exner 1997 The Beginnings of Winemaking and Viniculture in the Ancient Near East and Egypt. Expedition 39(1):3–21

[7] Zohary D, Hopf M. Domestication of Plants in the Old World: The Origin and Spread of Cultivated Plants in West Asia, Europe, and the Nile Valley. Oxford: Oxford Univ Press; 2000. Pp. 205–206; Murray, Mary Anne, 2000. Viticulture and wine production, in: Ancient Egyptian Materials and Technology. (eds. P. Nicholson and I. Shaw). Cambridge University Press, 577-608.

[8] P.E. Mc Govern, A. Mirzoian, G. R. Hall, 2009: Ancient Egyptian herbal wines, Proc Natl Acad Sci U S A. May 5; 106(18): 7361–7366. Published online 2009 Apr 13. Doi: 10. 1073/ pnas.0811578106

One of the oldest Egyptian certifications of crops grapevine is reported on a piecemeal list, dating back to the above-mentioned King Djoser (2600 BC), where we find a wine called "*Star of Horus in the height of heaven*". While under Ramses III we have a list of 513 different grape varieties, each with its own label that writes down the type of wine, the epithet of the vineyard, the epithet of the post, the date of collection, the epithet of the vintner and the certificate of character. It is the first registered designations of controlled origin like labels of quality certification that today we find on Italian wine bottles.

"Labels" are the most concrete evidence of what the Egyptians knew about the strengths and weaknesses of wine, which could change according the above-mentioned parameters. These documents are proof of the importance that wine had in the preparation of remedies, ointments, and tinctures. In fact, the Egyptian papyruses wine mention the main ingredients. According to different recipes, they recommend the use of aromatic wine, old wine, fine wine, or wine of the vineyard of a specific area or owner.

The advice to use old wine or wine ten years old suggests that Egyptians knew that the aging wine took on a different alcohol content, which was increasing year-by-year, turning into a versatile substance that can dissolve fats, resins, and vehicular essential oils, improving their quality and conservation. Almost all Egyptian recipes report wine as the main ingredient with which to start making ointments, and medications.

The process began with the boiling of animal fat in wine to remove the smell of meat, and acquire that of wine. The other ingredients, in specific proportions, were added in succession, depending on type, measure, and expected time for production. The process was interrupted several times, even for days, to give time for the amalgam to mature. In these phases of "rest", the alcohol contained in wine grew in intensity because of added sugars, stabilizing the composition.

The mixture should not boil, but only reach the correct temperature, which allowed the melting of resins, terpenes, and various fat components. Otherwise, the alcohol would evaporate. Wine was the osmotic agent, as it allowed the melting of ingredients. Along with olive oil, it had an extraordinary importance in the preparation of cosmetics, pharmaceutical remedies, and magic potions. Enolita or tincture is the name of the pharmaceutical preparation of wine, in which drugs and plants macerate to extract the active ingredients.

In Europe, the Galenic preparation of these tinctures became peculiar of pharmacies and the most famous monasteries that preserved old recipes. In the Near East and India, they are still widespread and used. The most renewed tinctures that still exist contains *wine, Boldo, China, Cascara Sagrada, Condurango* and *Rhubarb*.

Turning back to the title of this paper *"Cyprus in the prehistory of wine,"* we move our attention in the middle of the eastern Mediterranean, where the knowledge of winemaking reached Cyprus about the same period of Egypt, at the end of the 4th millennium BC. Presuming that the Mc Govern discovery of a wine at Hajji Firuz is correct (Fig.7), and that some of the first grape wines were produced in Iran, we could suppose that the knowledge of winemaking arrived in Cyprus following a millenarian caravan route, which connected the Mediterranean and the Persian Gulf.

Fig.7: Hajji Firuz (Armenia) biconical vase analysed by P. Mc Govern.

Accepting that wild grapes naturally grow widely on the island as in the continental countries around, where cultivation possibly started before, we should presume that in Cyprus grape cultivation met favourable climatic and weather conditions. Ignoring when the consumption of grapes started in the Neolithic period, we have chosen to connect the story of the Cyprus wine with its pottery typology, even if it is logical to presume that wine is more ancient than the invention of ceramics and that the first containers to store and transport wine were the wineskins (made of skin of sheep, Fig.8), mentioned, and represented in the entire iconographic Mediterranean repertoire.

Fig.8: Wineskin hung in an old house in Cyprus.

Wineskin is a container for safe and easy handling, employed in Europe, the Mediterranean and Cyprus until a few years ago, to transport the wine from the country to the city. Hung on the kitchen wall in a temporary store it supplies a quick disposal of wine for domestic use.

Its shape and dimension depends on many factors often linked to the size of the animal. The largest were made using the entire skin of the animal, trying to maintain it as intact as possible, knotting the skin on the legs and the tail and using the neck as an opening to pour wine in and out and closed normally by the same rope used for hanging it on the wall. It is interesting to notice that wineskin in Greek is called askos, a word attributed in the archaeological dictionary at vases of modest dimensions of animal shapes or adorned by an animal head (sometimes human), believed to represent the old wineskin used to serve wine.

The transition from the wineskin to a container made of ceramics must have faced many difficulties, as the wine is a living liquid, in continuous transformation, especially when it is just made. If the fermentation is still in process, the vase cannot be closed, but as soon as it ends the wine container must be sealed otherwise contact with the air will change it to vinegar. So gradually, the standard primitive jars used for every purpose in the Neolithic period took up a specific shape more suitable to store wine. First, the neck of the vase became more narrow and with a mouth hole to facilitate the tapping and the possibility to cover the liquid with olive oil or resin to prevent the oxygenation. Then, the vase assumed an elongated shape to collect the wine sediments at the bottom. If we compare the shape of the Hajji Firuz (Armenia) vase, where the most ancient wine 5th millennium BC was found, with the Egyptian and the Godin Tepe wine jars we can observe the evolution of the shape (Fig.9).

Fig.9: Evolution jars from *Hajji Firuz, Godin Tepe, Egypt, Erimi, Roma.*

Regarding Cyprus, we have evidence of consumption of grapes in the 5th millennium BC, as wild grape seeds have been found at the Neolithic site of Aghios Epikthesos-Vrisy (4500-3900 BC) in the district of Kyrenia[9]. They are possibly linked to the production of wine in the characteristic underground areas of the settlement. The same variety of wild grape seeds were found in the Chalcolithic (Paphos) village of Lemba Lakkous of the late 4th millennium BC[10].

Moving to the South along the seacoast, we find the large settlement of Erimi, which was inhabited without interruption of continuity from the 4th millennium BC until today[11]. The position of the site favoured permanent habitation, with a river and a valley connecting with the hinterland rich in minerals and ores, and fertile land. The geographical location of Erimi (Fig.10) made its inhabitants mediators between the western and eastern villages distributed along both sides of the Kouris River, as far as the inland mountain settlements.

The southern coast of Cyprus from the bay of Larnaka to the Akamas promontory was densely populated in the Neolithic period. Hence, the establishment of the first settlement at Choirokoitia (Khirokitia) should probably be linked with a smaller group of colonists who, in search of free farming land and pastures, left the coastal areas between Anatolia and Palestine and came to Cyprus. Although the settlement of these colonists was relatively long-lived, it is impossible to discover any new, specific expression for the study of their physical appearance and spiritual culture. The circular huts, grouped according to a system in the oldest settlements of Choirokoitia and Kalavasos were also adopted by the first Erimi inhabitants.

---

[9] M. Kyllo 1982. The Botanical Remains, in E. Peltenburg, *Vrysi, a Subterranean Settlement in Cyprus. Excavations at Prehistoric Ayios Wpiktitos Vrysi, 1969-1973*, Warminster.

[10] S. Colledge 1985. The Plant remains, in E. Peltenburg et al. *Lemba Archaeological Project vol. I. Excavations at Lemba -Lakkous, 1976-1983*, Gotemburg.

[11] Dikaios, P. 1939: Excavations at Erimi 1933-1935: Final Report, Report of the Department of Antiquities, Cyprus, 1-81.

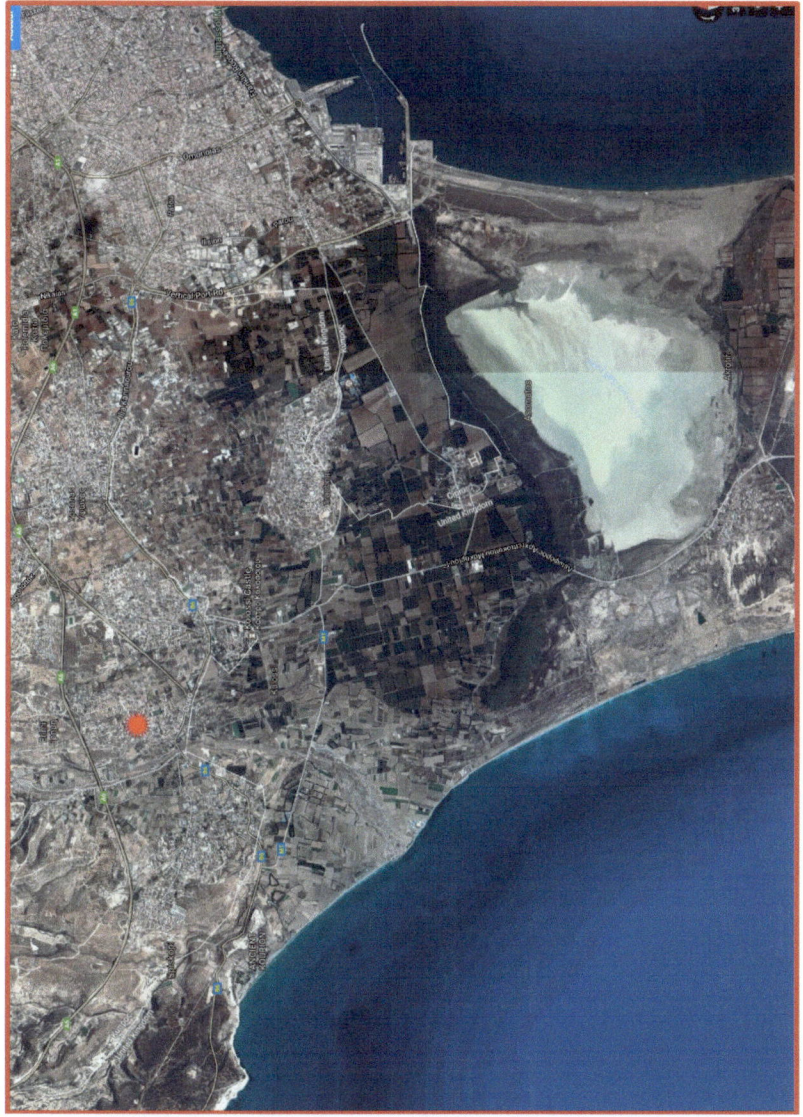

Fig.10: Geographical position of Erimi along the Kouris river.

The first pottery typology bears clear reference to the older models of stone; meanwhile the decoration indicates that the proponents of the Erimi culture maintained relations with the inhabitants of the inland areas and the coasts oversea[12].

---

[12] Bolger, D.L. 1988: Erimi Bamboula: a Chalcolithic Settlement in Cyprus, British Archaeological Reports International Series 443 (BAR, Oxford).

Available archaeological material implies that the first inhabitants of Erimi had good neighbourly relations both with the communities of the Kouris valley and of the southeaster part of the gulf of Lemesos (Limassol). The old settlement of Erimi was neither fenced nor fortressed, and the relics of its houses associate with the serene domestic living of the inhabitants, whose daily life consisted mainly in making stone tools and ceramics, preparing food, and tending their fields and animals (Fig.11).

Fig. 11: Erimi excavation of a Neolithic house in 1932.
Courtesy Department Antiquities of Cyprus

At the end of the Neolithic period, however, the population of the oldest settlement of Erimi moved from the first site, probably due to the upheaval caused by the competition on the first copper production and trade, towards the valley and by maritime communication.

The second settlement was arranged not far from the first along the riverside. Within the time span of a thousand years Erimi remained a village, with the same system of communication, but a different house distribution. Continuity of its culture is abundantly manifested in the tombs, and in the reuse of stone tools. The community of Bronze Age Erimi used to adapt their main activities to the local conditions. Thus, more attention was paid first to farming and stockbreeding and secondly to metallurgy.

This was not, however, due to the innovation of the Erimi inhabitants, but rather a consequence of new cultural knowledge that came from the continent and, pushed them to search for new materials and copper minerals. The discovery of metal upset the previous culture, changing the social relations based on the old traditions. The crisis generated by the introduction of metal, in a still predominantly agrarian environment, probably formed new classes, which contradicted the traditional way of life.

Significant evidence of material culture evolution mirrors itself in the number of the small archaeological sites distributed around the Kouris valley, inhabited since the Neolithic period[13]. The Erimi territory is unique in archaeological terms, due to the uninterrupted sequence of sites, including medieval monasteries and churches. .

Erimi was one of the first excavated Neolithic settlements in Cyprus (Dikaios 1932-35) (Fig.12).

Fig.12: Dikaios excavations at Erimi:
Courtesy Department Antiquities of Cyprus

The cultural layers of Erimi excavated by Dikaios, offer an unusually interesting stratigraphy of 11 floor remains, consisting of many

---

[13] Belgiorno M.R. Short 2005: Report of the First Survey Made at Erimi/Kafkalla (October 2004), RDAC, 225-231.

versatile objects: stone and bone tools and weapons, pottery for everyday use, decorated vases, some proto anthropomorphic figurines, and simple jewellery of bone, shell, and stone. Hundreds of items have been found in the tombs of the Early, Middle and Late Bronze Age, but most of these remain unpublished.

Moreover, little attention has been paid to the shape of the chalcolithic jars showing off a characteristic ovoidal shape on pointed base (for easy handling) and a cylindrical neck tapered towards the mouth. Although the type was still known in size not exceeding 35cm, the jars found by Dikaios were taller than 60 cm. (Fig.13).

Fig.13: Wine jar from the Neolithic village of Erimi

They were true proto-amphorae, white slip inside and outside, and decorated with wide brush strokes of red. The tapered shape and the poor handling of the jars (without handles or sockets, like the smaller examples), suggested that form had a functional purpose and therefore it had been intentional.

The comparison with other forms of the Chalcolithic vascular repertoire, characterized by wide flat bases, indicates a search in getting the pointed base, element that requires commitment and are not easy to master during the manufacture process.

History seems to rule out a possible derivation from the conical Egyptian jars and Armenian biconical without handles and vessels found at Godin Tepe (3200 B.C.). Furthermore, both Armenia and Cyprus preserved the shape to this day in the traditional "pithari", a sort of gigantic wine jar without handles, with the pointed base, to process and store wine (Fig.14).

Fig.14: Traditional "pithari" of XVIII and XIX centuries.

The chronology of the Erimi jars, established by the Department of Antiquities of Cyprus, swings between the half and the end of the 4th millennium BC, pointing to exclude that they could be a direct evolution of the Egyptian jars, at most contemporary. These observations suggested the hypothesis that the Erimi jars could be made intentionally by the Cypriot people to make wine.

In organising a possible Archaeometry investigation on them, we found that most of the pottery excavated by Dikaios was still fragmentary and unwashed inside their original boxes since the 1935, in the storage room of the Limassol District Museum.

In collaboration and under the permission of the Department of the Antiquities of Cyprus, the analyses of the original residues collected in the bottom of the vases were organised with the financial support and collaboration of the Italian Embassy in Nicosia, which organised a press conference to introduce the results achieved. In April 2005, the team of the Italian Archaeological Mission of the Institute for Technologies Applied to Cultural Heritage of the Italian CNR scratched and analysed the inside remains of 18 fragmentary bases of jars directly in the laboratories of Limassol and Nicosia Museum.

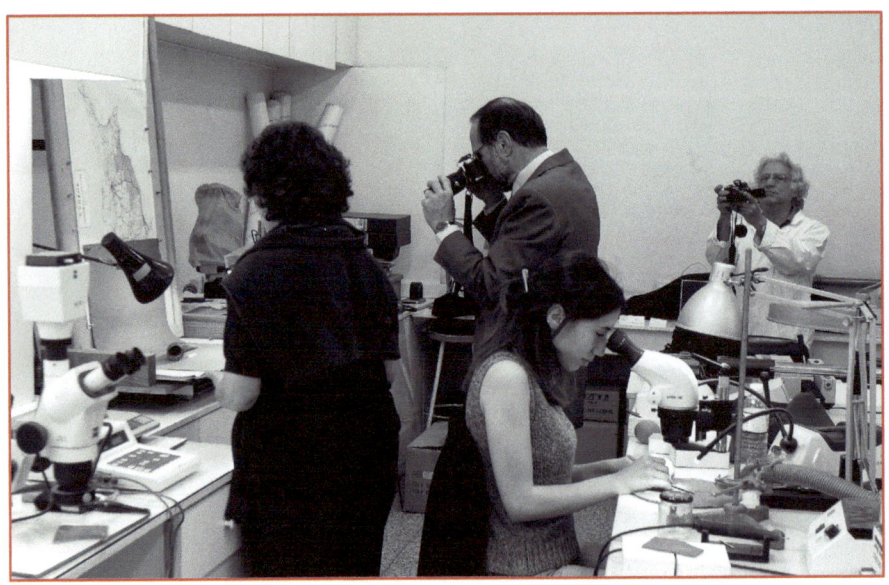

Fig.15: Documentation of the analyses in the laboratory of Nicosia Museum

De facto Alessandro Lentini performed the analyses, using Feigl test[14] to find traces of tartaric acid left of the wine in the bottom of the vases.

Few grams of material have been taken inside each base, dissolving in a solution of H_2SO_4 (20%).

After some minutes, the reaction disintegrated all the organic material, leaving only the racemase residual of tartaric acid. The β.β"-dinaftolo added to the supernatant gives to the composition the

---

[14] Feigl M.1989: Spot Test in Organic Analysis. Seventh Completely Revised Edition, Elseveir.Amsterdam.

property to become green under the Ultra Violet rays if the lamp is of 240-250 nanometres waves (Fig.16).

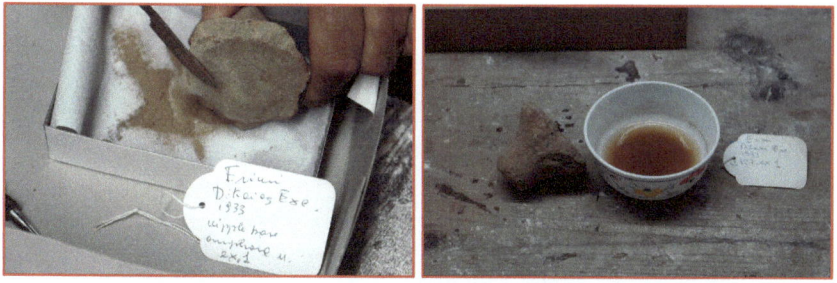

Fig. 16: Analysis and results under the UV Lamp of a sample.

The results demonstrated that 12 jar bottoms contained a large amount of tartaric acid (a characteristic acid of red wine), while six contained only traces of the same acid (see after Lentini). It was evident that the Chalcolithic pointed jars from Erimi have been used to process wine, positioning them at the beginning of the evolution of the wine amphora typology[15].

---

[15] M.R. Belgiorno 2009. Cinyra, Cyprus and the notes of music, of wine and perfumes, in *Notes of Kyniras Music, Wine and Perfume*, Cyprus Wine Museum Publications. Nicosia, 30-55; Belgiorno M.R. e Lentini A. 2010. Il vino di Erimi inquadramento storico e analisi archeometriche, In: *Researches in Cypriote History and Archaeology*, a cura di Jasink A.M. e Bombardieri L., Firenze University Press, Firenze, 175-182; M.R. Belgiorno & A. Lentini 2005. *Cyprus: 5000 years of wine civilisation*. Nicosia June 2005, Italian Embassy (ed.), Limassol; M.R. Belgiorno and A. Lentini 2012. Il vino più antico del Mediterraneo, in *Darwin*, 2012 n°47, 18 - 25.

The confirmation that the vases had contained wine made Cyprus one of the most ancient Mediterranean countries where wine was produced, and the place where the best ceramic shape, linked to a specific technology to ferment and clarify the wine had been perfected.

This is the biodynamic system, still adopted to produce top quality wines, which without the addition of selected yeasts, uses terracotta shaped containers for decanting wine. Considering that the vases were coming from dwellings and not tombs, the data acquired through the analysis testifies that the wine was fermented and stored at the end of the fourth millennium BC by people devoted to agriculture and farm breeding.

Fig.17: Analysis results of the askos (T.97 n. 277) from Souskiou.

Moreover, we may presume that the smaller versions of the wine jars, often found in the graves outfits, holding less than two litres, were used for domestic consumption of wine, and that the pointed base was necessary to collect the deposit of the liquid which probably had addition of herbs or other ingredients.

The type did not disappear during the Early and Middle Bronze age, and the pointed base for centuries remained an identification element of the wine jugs. Among the Chalcolithic vases coming from the territory around, Alessandro Lentini examined two more pots, which shape and painted decoration could be in connection to the wine.

They have been found in Chalcolithic tombs near Souskiou, a village few kilometres far from Erimi. The first has the shaped of a bunch of grapes (Fig.17) and the second is a bowl decorated with bunches of grapes painted under the rim.

Both testify to the importance that the grapes had taken in the agricultural economy of the time.

Furthermore, we should include in the number of Chalcolithic vases possibly linked with the production and consumption of wine an askos probably from a Chalcolithic-looted tomb of Souskiou, belonging to the collection Hadjiprodromou before the division of the island in 1974. Today the object is in the S. Barnaba Monastery Museum in Northern Cyprus.

Fig.18: Human head askos (Souskiou?), S. Barnaba Monastery Museum

The askos has a body shaped as the characteristic wine jars of Erimi, with the pointed base, four legs added on one side and a human head with the top open to be used as a pot. It is considered one of the most ancient representation of centaur and its practical linking with the wine suggests the existence of some earliest religious beliefs associated specifically with wine (Fig.18).

In this regard, I would like to remind that proof emergence and use of wine, indicating to the prehistoric production and consumption is the religious employ in which wine became a separate and important ritual component affecting the social evolution, the spiritual life, and the early differentiation of the deities. If we accept the theory that the winemaking was deeply connected to a deity with a distinct affinity to wine, we should identify in Cyprus the territory where an archetype of the wine god took probably shape around the end of the fourth millennium BC.

In fact, horns, grapes, snakes, and centaurs are all Cypriot elements and characters, which we find later relating to the Mediterranean myth of Dionysus, god of wine per antonomasia.

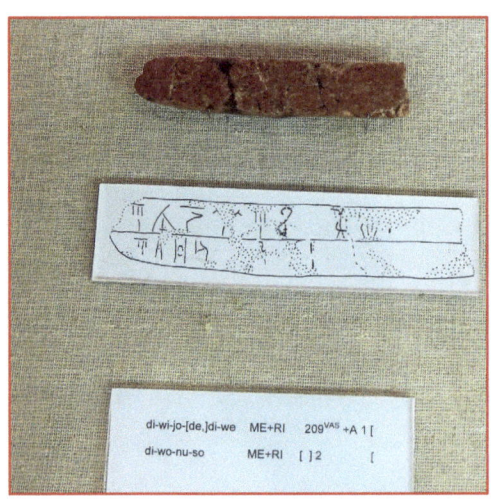

Fig. 19: Myc.B Tablet with "di-wo-nu-so" 1400BC, Chania Museum, Crete.

At his birth, with two horns on his forehead, we have two versions; the first (less following) from Crete relates the love of Zeus and Persephone in the form of a snake[16] the second relating Semele, daughter of Cadmus, king of Thebe and descendant of Io, loved by Zeus in the form of a bull[17].

---

[16] It happened in a cave near the spring of Kyane guarded by two snakes where Demetra had hidden the daughter Persephone Diodorus li. IV. Kerenyi, K. 1976. *Dionysus: Archetypal Image of Indestructible Life*. UK: Princeton University Press 111-116.

[17] Per Hesiod and Homer, Dionysius, the son of Zeus and Semele was born

Both versions suggest that the many decorations of snakes and the horns of the Cypriot Bronze Age repertoire, maybe in connection to the cult of wine.

Therefore, given the chronology of these symbolic apotropaic elements we cannot exclude the possibility that an archetype of Dionysus was worshipped in Cyprus before the beginning of the Bronze Age, evolving in parallel with the Minoan god of wine reported as "di-vo-no-so-Jo" in syllabic Mycenaean B in the 1400 BC tablets, found in the Minoan palace at Chania (Fig.19).

As often happens in the history, the myth may have been originated from real objects connected with wine, years before a divinity was conceived to attribute the invention of such a precious liquid to a superior being, as well as many other human discoveries.

Therefore, regarding the horns which seem to be an unquestioned characteristic of the god, we must remember that in Cyprus the horns are a decorated plastic element characteristic of all the Early/Middle Bronze age pottery, with examples dating back to the Neolithic period (Fig.20).

Fig. 20: 7000 BC Stone bowl with a horned handle from Kalavassos prehistoric village, on a Cypriot stamp.

Ox horns cut at the base, empty and cleaned up inside are perhaps the most ancient drinking vessels used until our days, whose

---

with two small horns on his forehead since, the mother, daughter of Cadmus, king of Thebe, was a descendant of Io, loved by Zeus resembling a heifer. Burkert, Walter, *Greek Religion*, 1985, 64, 132; Kerenyi, above cited.

employment logically followed the presence of the bovine on the land and their taming.

Fig.21: Palaeolithic Venus Laussel 20000 BC, Musée d'Aquitaine Bordeaux.

Its perishability however has left no traces of its use in remote times, but we can presume that in some areas it was used since the Neolithic period. Moreover, from the etymology studies, we know that the word ceramic (pottery) which identifies the objects made of fired clay probably came from the Greek word Keras that means horn, as recently reaffirmed by Seal and Baraton[18]

"The word ceramics comes from the Greek keras, horn. In prehistoric times, horns were used as containers; later ceramic containers made out of clay were used to store food, water, wine, oil. Ceramic describes the working of the clay. The hardening of the clay under the hot desert sun may have given our ancestors the idea that clay would harden even more if subjected to fire. It was the right understanding, and since then ceramics have been part of human civilization".

---

[18] S. Seal and M.I. Baraton 2004: "Toward Applications of Ceramic Nanostructures", MRS Bulletin January.

The clay horn appears in the pottery repertoire of Cyprus in Early Bronze age and was found among funeral goods, especially in the tombs of Vounous in the Kyrenia district.

Their use for drinking wine was confirmed by our analyses (Fig.22).

Fig.22: Analysis of a clay horn from Vounous T.164 n°61.

However, the drinking horns was not an exclusive Cypriote product in 2000 BC. We find examples almost contemporary in Palestine and Egypt[19].

In turn, its presence in Cyprus confirms the extensive consumption of wine, suggesting that during the Bronze Age production of wine

---

[19] D. Namdar, R. Neumann, Y. Goren, and S. Weiner 2009. The contents of unusual cone-shaped vessels (cornets) from the Chalcolithic of the southern Levant, *Journal of Archaeological Science* 36, 629-636.

took on importance, affecting the social relations and aggregation of people. It was so important that we find representations of the making of wine in figurative compositions of the Early and Middle Bronze age. The repertoire, rich in coroplastic representations, often narrates moments of rural and domestic life with rare expressions of worship.

The most significant is a model of crushing vat, probably from a looted tomb of Vounous, and a double-necked jug from the tomb 36 of Pyrgos. The first one is a "Red Polished" model from the antiquary market[20], purchased by the Leventis Foundation of Cyprus in the Christie's auction of the Desmond Morris Cypriot antiquities collection.

Fig.23: Grape pressing model 2000/1-25, Archaeological Museum Nicosia

---

[20] D. Morris 1985. *The Art of Ancient Cyprus*, Oxford, 279.

The representation articulates around a sort of oval tub, resting on four legs, with a large side spout. Eleven people take part in the scene.

One figure, inside the vat, is bigger than the others are. Around, six people are standing outside in a symmetrical position attending the scene, and another four seem to support and control the opening of the vat, which is represented sloping downwards (Fig. 23)[21].

The scenic vase has a comparison with a proto-dynastic pressing model from the necropolis of Abydos in Egypt. In this case, eight people are standing around the rim of the vat (Fig. 24).

Fig.24: Protodynastic pressing model from Abydos, Cairo Museum

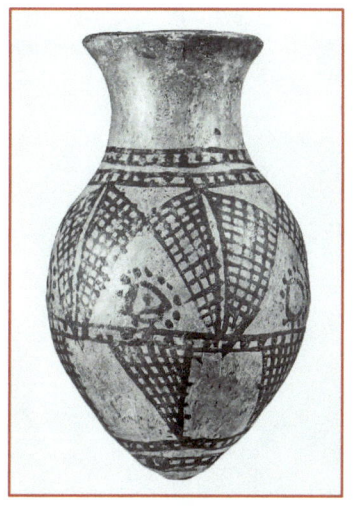

Fig.25: Cypriot Chalcolithic wine jar from the antiquary market.

A similar subject may be symbolised in the painted decoration of a small chalcolithic wine jar from Cyprus, unfortunately from a looted tomb, where a line of people holding a rim seems represented around the body. On the upper register of the decoration, there are five twin groups of drinking horns (Fig.25).

The second, a double-necked jug from the tomb 36 of Pyrgos is considered the masterpiece of the Middle Bronze Age coroplastic

---

[21] Karageorghis V. & Belgiorno M.R. 2005: Primi esempi di tecnologie agricole e industriali nell'Età del Bronzo a Cipro. CNR. Roma.

Cypriot art. It is a large jug with a double spouted mouth, decorated on the shoulder with a glimpse of rural life focused on the crushing of grapes[22]. Many figurines of men, women, children, and animals compose the scenic vase, all attending at the wine making.

Fig.26: Double neck scenic jug from Pyrgos, with grape pressing. Archaeological Museum Limassol

The representation turns around the figure positioned at the top between the two necks, engaging in foot treading grapes in an oval vat

---

[22] Flourentzos P. 2001: Recent Rare Finds related to the Cult and Everyday Life in Early/Middle Bronze Age Cyprus, 159-166 in A. Kyriatsoulis (ed) Kreta und Zypern. Religion und Schrift, Ohlstadt.

furnished with a large spout from which the liquid is intended to be collected in a large bowl (Fig.26).

The person centrepiece of the performance is a naked woman arranged in a figurative theme, already known for the Egyptian Pre-dynastic period (compare the model from a tomb of Naqada depicting a girl in a vat Fig. 27).

In this case, the subject is enriched by a coroplastic agricultural environment in which the characteristic spectacular taste of the Cyprus Middle Bronze Age expresses its trend towards the choral organization and sociality. Both the specimens are among the most ancient representation of wine making realized in clay.

Fig.27: Model from a Predynastic tomb of Naqada, Cairo Museum

The restitution of the drinking horns in ceramics, copying the real dimension and shape of the horn could be also related to apotropaic beliefs, tied to the sacrality of the bull; a symbol of power and fertility in the entire Mediterranean horizon. In fact, the unique evidence of a Cypriot cult dating back to the Early Bronze age is three clay models representing totemic sanctuaries with three pillars surmounted of horned heads (Fig.28) from the E-MBA tombs of Kochati, Nicosia.

Fig.28: Shrine Models from Kochati,

In historical times, from the symposium scenes represented in the Greek painting and in the Etruscan tombs we know that the use of the simple cattle drinking horn continues to be widely used.

Fig.29: Sgraffito ware wedding dish with drinking horn and wine jug.

Its use did not pass out fashion in the next periods, since the Romans spread its use to the Northern countries together with their conquests.

Today we find the drinking horn in most of European convivial traditions including the Russian ones, realized in poor and precious materials in thousands of examples.

Still in Cyprus, the drinking horns remained in traditional use as documented by the wedding medieval representation of the "*sgraffito ware*" dishes and cups (Fig.29). They have been used without solution of continuity because even today the country tradition will conserve the memory of use, especially during the festivities and on the wine festivals organized to welcome the new wine.

You can find more evidence of their relative recent use in the wine house-museums located in the villages producing wine, together with the father and grandfather wine equipment used till 50 years ago, comprising goat wine-skins, pumpkin funnels, and ladles, and old *pitharka*, jealously conserved.

In wine villages of Cyprus, it is also possible to see ancient "Linos", which are squared stone built vats to tread the grapes, positioned under a large opening in the roof from where it was possible to throw down the grapes. A hole on the bottom of the vat on the wall allowed the liquid to be collected after the fermentation and transferred in large pyriform jars positioned all around.

This equipment is not far from those used in prehistoric times represented on a Pyrgos' scenic vase found in a tomb from the 19th century BC. The circular vat of treading grapes is still one of the most used home wine equipment in Europe, but in Cyprus rare examples survive in their original context.

In southern Italy, however, hundreds of examples survive outdoors and indoors known as the wine *palmenti*, and the jars used to process and store wine are the huge *capasoni*.

In Cyprus, one of the most ancient *linos* is located at Erimi in the Aghios Georghios cave not far from the village, and has been recently reopened and cleaned (Fig.30).

Fig.30: Linos in the Aghios Georghios' cave, Erimi.

The entrance of Aghios Georghios "linos" was sealed with large stones around the XIV century, when Erimi suffered a kind of wine *damnatio memory* and today the village, from which comes one of the most ancient Mediterranean wines, and the most ancient examples of wine jars, no longer has any vineyard or wine production.

In any case, wine fermented and ageing in clay jars is no longer produced in Cyprus. It is still produced in Italy, Georgia, and Armenia according to a renewed taste in biodynamic system, using terracotta amphora of 250 to 400 litres, and without the use of selected yeasts.

In Georgia and Armenia still survive the system of burying the wine jars (called *kvevri*) under the floor of the houses, covered only by a slab of stone as in the old Cypriot tradition that goes back to the Late Bronze Age. Georgian/Armenian tradition has more in common with Cyprus, as the wine is still drunk in animal horns named *"kantsi"* (embroidered deer, bull or goat horn passed around the table), and the grapes-must is used to produce the *coucouko*, as in Cyprus.

Moreover, the industrial complex of Pyrgos, dating back to the Early and Middle Bronze age, has furnished several pots relating to the production and consumption of the wine, as well as seeds and pollen of *Vitis silvestris* and *sativa* (see after Archaeometry by A. Lentini).

The repertoire includes jars, jugs, and two interesting amphorae whose shape anticipates that of the Mycenaean wine krater (Fig.31), which will appear after centuries among the drinking outfit for the symposium[23].

Fig. 31: Wine Proto krater, Pyrgos/Mavroraki n°. 466, Limassol Museum.

---

[23] Steel L. 2004: A goodly cup of mellow wine; Feasting in Bronze Age Cyprus, in *Hesperia* 73, 281-300.

Among the jars, we found a characteristic storage jar with the pointed base and a rich decoration of impressed necklaces of grapes (Fig.32) close to the fragments of two apparatuses for distillation[24]. Amid the fragments of the alembics and jar (which have been completely restored by Lavinia de Strobel), there were more bowls, basins, and many seeds of grapes.

Fig.32: Wine storage jar from Pyrgos/Mavroraki, n. 355 Limassol Museum

---

[24] Belgiorno M.R. 2016: The Perfume of Cyprus, Roma, 188, fig. 118.

The assembly leaves open the hypothesis that not only the plants, but also the pomace could have been distilled to produce pharmacological compounds and fragrances[25]. Still analysed by Alessandro Lentini, remains of tartaric acid have been found in this jar and in two pointed base jugs coming from the rooms around (Lentini, Fig.10). Two other pots from Pyrgos/Mavroraki are possibly connected with the wine, as they bear plastic decorations of Dionysian symbols consisting in small taurine heads and snakes. The jug n° 423 is 47, 5 cm high with a very elegant long, narrow and spouted neck, and decoration formed by a mixture of incised geometric motifs and applied plastic elements.

Fig.33: Jug with bucrania and snakes from Pyrgos/Mavroraki n. 423.

---

[25] Belgiorno M.R. 2016: Chap. 7, Distillation. in *The Perfume of Cyprus*, Rome.

Small taurine heads and snakes are applied to the body enriched by the incision of vertical lines running up to the mouth (Fig.33).

The jug n° 107 is 50cm high; the peculiarity of this vase consists not only in the elongated and elegant shape, conferred by the long spout and the precious woven handle, but also in the complex incised and applied decoration (Fig.34).

Fig.34: Jug with human figure and snakes, Pyrgos/Mavroraki n. 107

The whole composes an elaborate symbolism, where two snakes are represented on both sides of a human figure; meanwhile a third snake interlaces it. The human figurine stands on the front body below the neck, with the head positioned on the base of the neck.

The hairs are represented by wavy lines incised running down to the sides of the long neck / body of the figurine, up to the snake in relief crossing horizontally across the body of the figure above its legs.

Another two snakes in relief are arranged vertically in heraldic position, flanked symmetrically to the figure, descending from the base neck to the body of the vase. On the neck, exactly over the human figurine, there are three perforated rings arranged at regular intervals and connected by a zigzag decoration.

They climb on the beak of the amphora up to the last snake in relief, which on the front, marks the transverse cut of the beak' on the extreme top. Even if the snake is a recurrent decorative motive of Red Polished ware of Southern Cyprus, this association with a human figure is unique.

The principal allegory that reminds the Minoan version of the birth of Dionysus from Persephone and Zeus, who took the shape of a snake to enter the cave guarded by two snakes and love the daughter of Demetra[26].

From Cyprus, we also have one of the oldest examples of the use of taurine masks already at the beginning of the Bronze Age.

One anthropo-theriomorphic figure is incised on the side of an Early Bronze age "tulip vases" discovered in a tomb of the necropolis of Vounous[27].

---

[26] Kerényi K. 1963: *Gli dei e gli eroi della Grecia, gli Dei*, Roma. 208-214.
[27] Tulip-bowl, Vounous, Nec. A, Tomb 91 n. 14; Fitzwilliam Museum Cambridge, Inv. n. GR.5Y-1939; Woudhuysen P. 1982. *Treasures of the Fitzwilliam Museum*. Cambridge (Cambs.): Pevensey Press. 182; Karageorghis, V. 1993: *The coroplastic art of ancient Cyprus*. XI.3 p.151 pl. CXIV: 1; Stewart, E. Stewart, J. 1950: *Vounous 1937-38. Field-report on the Excavations Sponsored by the British School of Archaeology at Athens*. 97 no. 14, pls. lxxix,c-d, lxxx,a-b, xci,d, xciii,a,c-d, i,b; Karageorghis V., Vassilika E., Wilson P. 1999: *Art of Ancient Cyprus in the Fitzwilliam Museum, Cambridge*. Nicosia: 2-3 cat no. 3.

An unusual plastic decoration characterized the vessel on the rim, it consists of a series of solar discs alternating a bull, a bird, and ram heads, which seem to refer to the masks worn by the character represented on the pot. A similar figure is incised on an amphora from the same necropolis[28] (Fig. 35). Moreover, its iconography recalls that of a Minoan gem[29] (Fig. 36).

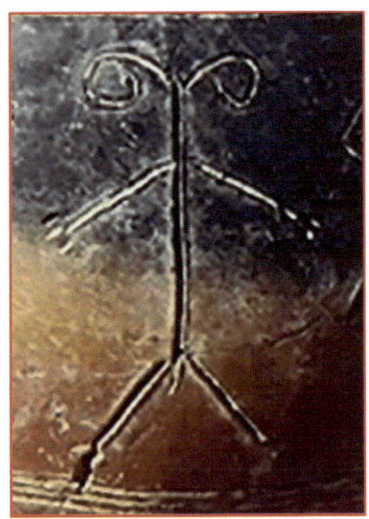

Fig.35: Cyprus Early Bronze Age Tulip- bowl from Vounous T.91 n.14, Fitzwilliam Museum Cambridge.

Fig.36: Minoan gem Middle Minoan I: Cabinet des medailles, Paris: CMS-IX-009-1

---

[28] Tomb 160 A, n. 16, Stewart, E. & Stewart, J. 1950. *Vounous 1937-38,* 201-209 pl. L: a.
[29] Förtsch R., von Hesberg H., Müller W., Pini I. 2011: *Corpus of Minoan and Mycenaean Seals,* volume: IX no. 9, Pars Cabinet des medailles, Paris: CMS-IX-009- 1, steatite.

From Vounous we have a clay model of the Early Bronze age, representing a religious ceremony celebrated within a circular structure. On its wall, three stylized human figures with taurine heads and snakes in the hands appear. Many people converge towards them, including a person sitting on a kind of throne[30].

On the religious significance of this model, it has been extensively argued: the scholars follow in general the first interpretation of Dikaios that considers the object a model of sanctuary where people are holding a religious ceremony[31].

In any case the essence of the Minoan myth could be summarized in the mystical formula known from Christian texts: "*taurus draconem genuit et taurum draco*": the bull is the father of the snake and the snake of bull (Arnobius, Adversus nationes V 21; Firmicus Maternus, De Errore XXVI, I).

In Cyprus, reminders of the ancient cult of Dionysus survive in the Aiora festival, which until the half of the last century involved all the families of Cyprus for four days around the end of February.

The Cypriot wine festival was linked to the engagement of the young girls who were in search of a husband. The family, which possessed a pointed arch in front of their house use to hang a swing during the Anthesteria days for their girls, while a traditional song followed the movement of the Aiora[32]. (Apollodorus Bibl. 3.14.7; Hyginus. Fa b. 130). The Athenian virgins also started to hang themselves from trees until Erigone's ghost was appeased by the establishment of the festival

---

[30] P. Warren, «Minoan Crete and Ecstatic Religion. Preliminary observations on the 1979 excavations at Knossos», in *Sanctuary and Cults in the Aegean Bronze Age* in Proc. Inter. Symp. Swed. Inst. Ath., 12-13 May 1980, Stockholm 1981.
[31] P. Dikaios, The Excavations at Vounous Bellapais in Cyprus 1931-32, *Archaeologia* 88, 1938, 1-174;
[32] There may be some connection between the Athenian festival of 'Swings' and the Roman custom of the 'Little Masks' in honour of Bacchus: G. Thaniel: 1976: Nodum Informis Leti, A-Class-19:77-81.80, n. 22; name of song in honor of Erigone, Ath.14.618e, Poll.4.55, Hsch.s.v.; cf. "ἑώρα" 11.

of 'Swings', at which a song called "the wanderer's song" was sung in memory of Erigone (Athen. 14.618 e) and small images were suspended in her honor from trees. Erigone, who is mentioned in association with Dionysus-Liber by Ovid (Metamorphoses 6: 125) was placed after her death in the constellation of Virgo.

Fig.37: Paphos: House of Dionysus: IIIAD Mosaic with Ikarios.

In the classical period, the Aiora took place on the last day of the Anthesteria, the Festival of Flowers, which honoured the god Dionysus and celebrated the year's vintage. It was a three-day festival, occurring around February 25th-27th.

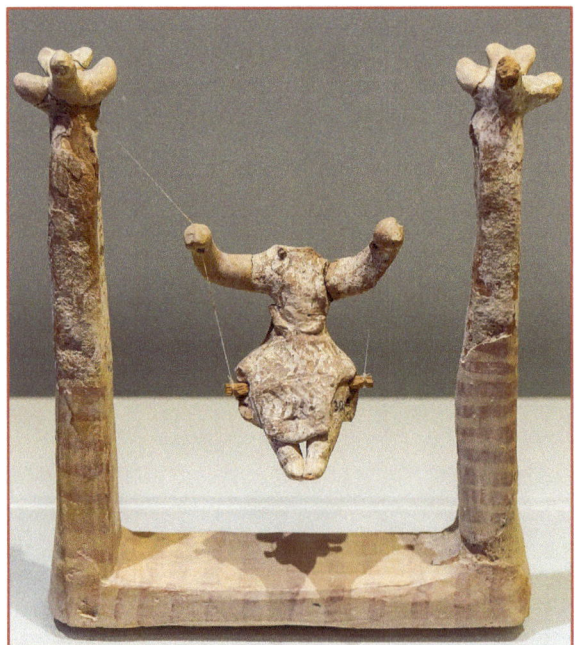

Fig.38: Aghia Triada model of girl on swing: Iraklion Museum Crete.

On the first day of the festival, the jars of wine from the previous year's harvest were opened. The statue of Dionysus was carried to his temple, and offerings were made. On the second day, all temples (except Dionysus) were closed, and the dead were then free to take part in the earthly celebrations. Everyone drank wine. Lots of wine.

The last day of the celebration commemorated the death of Erigone. She was the daughter of king Ikarios, who brought viticulture to Athens, and was killed by villagers who became drunk from drinking wine, and thought they have been poisoned (Fig.37).

When Erigone found the body of the father then she hanged herself from the tree under which her father lay. Girls on swings purify the vintage from this tragic murder.

The Aiora are extensively represented in the Attic vases, but the first representation of a girl on the swing comes from Aghia Triada, Crete (Fig.38). It is a Minoan model composed by a figurine of a young woman seated on a swing, which may testify that the Aiora wine festival linked with god Dionysus originated in Crete and dates back to the II millennium BC.

REFERENCES

-Barnard H, A.N. Dooley, G. Areshian, B. Gasparyan, and K.F. Faull 2011: Chemical Evidence for Wine Production Around 4000 BCE in the Late Chalcolithic Near Eastern Highlands, in *Journal of Archaeological Science* 38: 977–984.

-Belgiorno M.R. 2016: *The Perfume of Cyprus: from Pyrgos to François Coty the route of a legendary charm*, (ed.sc. Ermes) Rome.

-Belgiorno M.R. & A. Lentini 2005: *Cyprus: 5000 years of wine civilisation*. Nicosia June 2005, Italian Embassy (ed.), Limassol.

-Belgiorno M.R. 2005: Short Report of the First Survey Made at Erimi/Kafkalla (October 2004), *RDAC*, 225-231.

-Belgiorno M.R. 2009: Cinyra, Cyprus and the notes of music, of wine and perfumes, in *Notes of Kyniras Music, Wine and Perfume*, Cyprus Wine Museum Publications. Nicosia, 30-55.

-Belgiorno M.R. e Lentini A. 2010: Il vino di Erimi inquadramento storico e analisi archeometriche, In: *Researches in Cypriote History and Archaeology*, a cura di Jasink A.M. e Bombardieri L., Firenze University Press, Firenze, 175-182.

-Belgiorno M.R. and A. Lentini 2012: Il vino più antico del Mediterraneo, in *Darwin*, n°47, 18 - 25.

-Bolger D.L. 1988: Erimi Bamboula: QA Chalcolithic Settlement in Cyprus, British Archaeological Reports International Series 443 (*BAR*, Oxford).

-Burkert W. 1985: *Greek Religion*; Harvard University Press.

-Colledge S. 1985: The Plant remains, in E. Peltenburg et al. *Lemba Archaeological Project vol. I. Excavations at Lemba -Lakkous, 1976-1983*, Gotemburg.

-D'Ancona C. 1881: Gli antenati della vite vinifera, in *Atti della Regia Accademia dei Georgofili*, XIII.

-Dikaios P. 1938: The Excavations at Vounous Bellapais in Cyprus 1931-32, *Archaeologia* 88, 1938, 1-174.

-Dikaios P. 1939: *Excavations at Erimi* 1933-1935: *Final Report*, R.D.A.C., 1-81.

-Flourentzos P. 2001: Recent Rare Finds related to the Cult and Everyday Life in Early/Middle Bronze Age Cyprus, 159-166 in A. Kyriatsoulis (ed) *Kreta und Zypern. Religion und Schrift*, Ohlstadt.

-Förtsch R., von Hesberg H., Müller W., Pini I. 2011: *Corpus of Minoan and Mycenaean Seals*, volume: IX no. 9.

-Handwerk B. 2009: Scorpion King's Wines Egypt's Oldest, Spiked with Meds, in *National Geographic News* April 13.

-Karageorghis V. 1993: *The coroplastic art of ancient Cyprus*. Vol.1. Leventis Foundation, Nicosia.

-Karageorghis V., Vassilika E., Wilson P. 1999: *Art of Ancient Cyprus in the Fitzwilliam Museum, Cambridge*. Nicosia.

-Karageorghis V. & Belgiorno M.R. 2005: *Primi esempi di tecnologie agricole e industriali nell'Età del Bronzo a Cipro*. CNR. Roma.

-Kerényi K. 1963: *Gli dei e gli eroi della Grecia, gli Dei,* Roma.

-Kerenyi K. 1976: *Dionysus: Archetypal Image of Indestructible Life*. UK: Princeton University Press.

-Kyllo M. 1982: The Botanical Remains, in E. Peltenburg, *Vrysi, a Subterranean Settlement in Cyprus. Excavations at Prehistoric Ayios Wpiktitos Vrysi, 1969-1973*, Warminster.

-Mc Govern P.E., J.S. Fleming and S.H. Katz 1995: *The Origins and Ancient History of Wine*, New York and Luxembourg.

-Mc Govern P. E., U. Hartung, V. R. Badler, D. L. Glusker, and L. J. Exner 1997: The Beginnings of Winemaking and Viniculture in the Ancient Near East and Egypt. *Expedition* 39(1):3–21.

-Mc Govern P.E., A. Mirzoian, G., R. Hall, 2009: *Ancient Egyptian herbal wines*, Proc Natl Acad Sci U S A. May 5; 106(18): 7361–7366. Published online Apr 13. Doi: 10. 1073/ pnas.0811578106.

-Morris D. 1985: *The Art of Ancient Cyprus*, Oxford.

-Murray M.A. 2000: Viticulture and wine production, in: *Ancient Egyptian Materials and Technology*. (eds. P. Nicholson and I. Shaw). Cambridge University Press, 577-608.

-Myles S., A.R. Boyko, C.L. Owens, P.J. Brown, F. Grassi, M.K. Aradhya, B. Prins, B. Reynolds, A. Chiah, J.M. Wareh, D. Bustamante and E.S. Buckler 2011: *Genetic structure and domestication history of the grape*, Agricultural Sciences, Washington University 1, 6; Proceedings of the National Academy of Sciences.

-Namdar D., R. Neumann, Y. Goren, and S. Weiner 2009: The contents of unusual cone-shaped vessels (cornets) from the Chalcolithic of the southern Levant, *Journal of Archaeological Science* 36, 629-636;

-National Geographic Magazine, January 2011.

-Popov M.G. 1929: Dikie plodovye dereb'ja i kustarniki Srednej Azii.Trud. Poprikl, in *Botanike*, XXII, 3. 241-483.

-Schiemann E. 1953: Vitis in Neolithicum der Mark Brandenburg, in *Züchter*, XXIII, 1-11, 318-327.

-Seal S. & M.I. Baraton 2004: Toward Applications of Ceramic Nano Structures, *MRS Bulletin* January.

-Steel L. 2004: A goodly cup of mellow wine; feasting in Bronze Age Cyprus, in *Hesperia* 73, 281-300.

-Stewart, E. Stewart, J. 1950: *Vounous 1937-38. Field-report on the Excavations Sponsored by the British School of Archaeology at Athens.*

-Stummer A. 1911: Zur Urgeschichte der Reben und des Weinbaues, in *Mitteilungen der Anthropologischen Gesellschaft* in *Wien, 61,* 238296.

-Thaniel G. 1976: Nodum Informis Leti, *A-Class*-19: 77-81.

-Vavilov N. 1930: Wild Progenitors of the Fruit Trees of the Turkistan and the Caucasus and the Problem of the Origin of the Fruit Trees, IX *International Horticulture Congress London,* 271-286.

-Warren P. 1981: Minoan Crete and Ecstatic Religion. Preliminary observations on the 1979 excavations at Knossos, in *Sanctuary and Cults in the Aegean Bronze Age* in Proc. Inter. Symp. Swed. Inst. Ath., 12-13 May 1980, Stockholm.

-Wilkinson K.N., B. Gasparian, R. Pinhasi, P. Avetisyan, R. Hovsepyan, D. Zardaryan, G.E. Areshian, G. Bar-Oz and A. Smith 2012: Areni-1 Cave, Armenia: A Chalcolithic–Early Bronze Age settlement and ritual site in the southern Caucasus, in *Journal of Field Archaeology* vol. 37 N°1, 20-33.

- Woudhuysen P. 1982. *Treasures of the Fitzwilliam Museum.* Cambridge (Cambs.): Pevensey Press.

. Zohary D., Hopf M. 2000: Domestication of Plants in *The Old World: The Origin and Spread of Cultivated Plants in West Asia, Europe, and the Nile Valley.* Oxford: Oxford Univ Press, 205–206.

ARCHAEOMETRY INVESTIGATION
Alessandro Lentini

- Philogenesis of the Vitis during the Holocene

At the end of the Cenozoic, the primitive *Vitis* was hermaphrodite, similar to the present one[33]. In the phylogenetic evolution, the genetic hermaphroditic characters of the grapes became more clear (stamens plus anthers (male) which contain pollen, pistils with the ovary (female) for the development of seeds in the same flower.

The advantages of this evolutionary line that facilitates the reproduction are obvious. During the Quaternary glaciations the wild grape, due to the difficult climatic conditions, became dioecious in the area of provenance[34] and the genders became separate on various plants.

Every individual still had stamen and pistils in the flowers, but in

---

[33] Rögl F., 1999. *Oligocene and Miocene Palaeogeography and Stratigraphy of the CircumMediterranean Region*, (eds.) Whybrow P. J. and Hill A., vol. I, 485-500, Yale University Press, New Haven

[34] Nùñez D.G. and Walker M.J., 1989. 'A rewiev of paleobotanical finding of early Vitis in the Mediterranean and of the origin of cultivated grape-vines with special reference to new pointers to Prehistoric exploitation in the Western Mediterranean', *Rewiev of Palaeobotany and Palynology*, 61, 205-237

the males, maturation of one gene in the 38 chromosomes of the genetic equipment inhibited the development of the feminine organ (Su^F). In the females, the beginning of a recessive maturation prevented the development of the male stamen (the Su^M)[35].

In these conditions, the crossing pollination is more difficult, as it must be helped from other external factors (insects or atmospheric agents). In the dioecious shapes the male plant very rarely produces fruits, while the feminine fruit has a significant variation (morph Biometry, aspect, sugar level, proteins, acidity) caused by the genetic polymorphism of the plant.

Normally the modern wild Euro-Asiatic grapes produce small bitter fruits with many seeds, unsuitable for wine production. The sugar level is low, while the acidic level is very high. The skin of the fruit is hard and dark black-red coloured, very rarely it is white[36]. On the other hand, the cultivated Euro-Asiatic grapes show variable morpho-biometric characteristics, which are difficult to quantify. The grape can be of different dimensions with oblong or spherical morphology, and the anthocyanin colorations cover nearly all the chromatic spectrum. The level of sugar, acids and other less important chemical compounds have a well-known variability[37].

The domestication probably happened after selecting the plants at the primitive hermaphrodite level[38], showing regular and systematic fruit production, except for the dioecious plants.

---

[35] Walbot W. & Cullis C.A. 1983: The plasticity of the plant genome. Is it a requirement for success? Plant Molecular Biology Report 1, 3-14.
[36] Vavilov N. 1950: The origin, variation, immunity and breeding of cultivated plants, Trsld. by Starr K Chester. Chronica Botanicae, 13, XVII, 364.
[37] Maxted N., Ford-Loyd B.V. & Havkes J.G. 1997: Plant Genetic Conservation, Champman & Hall, London.
[38] Zohary D. & Hoff M., 2000, Domestication of Plants in the Old Wold: The Origin and Spread of Cultivated Plants in West Asia, Europe and the Nile Valley, Oxford, University Press.

- Geographic distribution

The wild Euro-Asiatic grapes occupies an area, which extends for about 6000 square Km, from Central Asia to Spain, and for about 1200 Km from Western Africa to Northern Crimea[39].

- Trans Caucasus region.

The Russian botanist Vavilov[40], who founded the modem Geobotany and Biodiversity, discovered some of the possible areas of origin and spread of the grape in Georgia, Armenia, and Azerbaijan. Such a wide area that extends from the Black Sea to the Caspian Sea (Fig.1) is dominated by the Caucasus Mountain, which is a natural barrier between Europe and Asia.

Between the Kura and Arakas rivers, large valleys with a mild climate dominate its geomorphology, which seems to provide the environmental conditions suitable for the cultivation of grape[41].

The 2004-2008 archaeological excavations turned up 41 whole seeds of different varieties of grapes (Tables 1-4) and several pedicel fragments, in Stratigraphic Units (SUs) PY04F8L1, PY05GH9L4/5, PY05L4 and PY06L5/2. All these seeds were found near pottery vessels (classified typologically as wine containers).

The 2004-2008 archaeological excavations turned up 41 whole seeds of different varieties of grapes (Tables 1-4) and several pedicel fragments, in Stratigraphic Units (SUs) PY04F8L1, PY05GH9L4/5, PY05L4 and PY06L5/2. All these seeds were found near pottery vessels (classified typologically as wine containers).

- The Mediterranean Region

One of the still unsolved problems regards the origin of the cultivated grapes and their genetic relationship with the wild grapes.

Per Levadoux, the modern grapes cultivated in Europe result from the Quaternary glacial pulsations towards the Southern

---

[39] Unwin T. 1991: Wine and the Vine: An Historical Geography of Viticulture and the Wine Trade, Books News, Portland.
[40] Vavilov N. 1950: The origin, variation, immunity and breeding of cultivated plants, Trsld. by Starr K Chester. Chronica Botanicae, 13, XVII, 364.
[41] Lisitsina G.N. & Walker M.J. 1989: The Caucasus: A Centre of Ancient Farm in Eurasia. In: Plants and Ancient Man, in Palaeoethnobotany, (eds.) Van Zeist W. & Casparie M.A., 285-292, A.A. Balkema, Amsterdam - Boston.

Mediterranean, including the great peninsulas and the great islands (Sicily, Sardinia, Cyprus, Crete, and Corsica), and Northern Africa (Rogl, 1999). This hypothesis partly differs from Vavilov's opinion that assumes a single origin for all the grapevines.

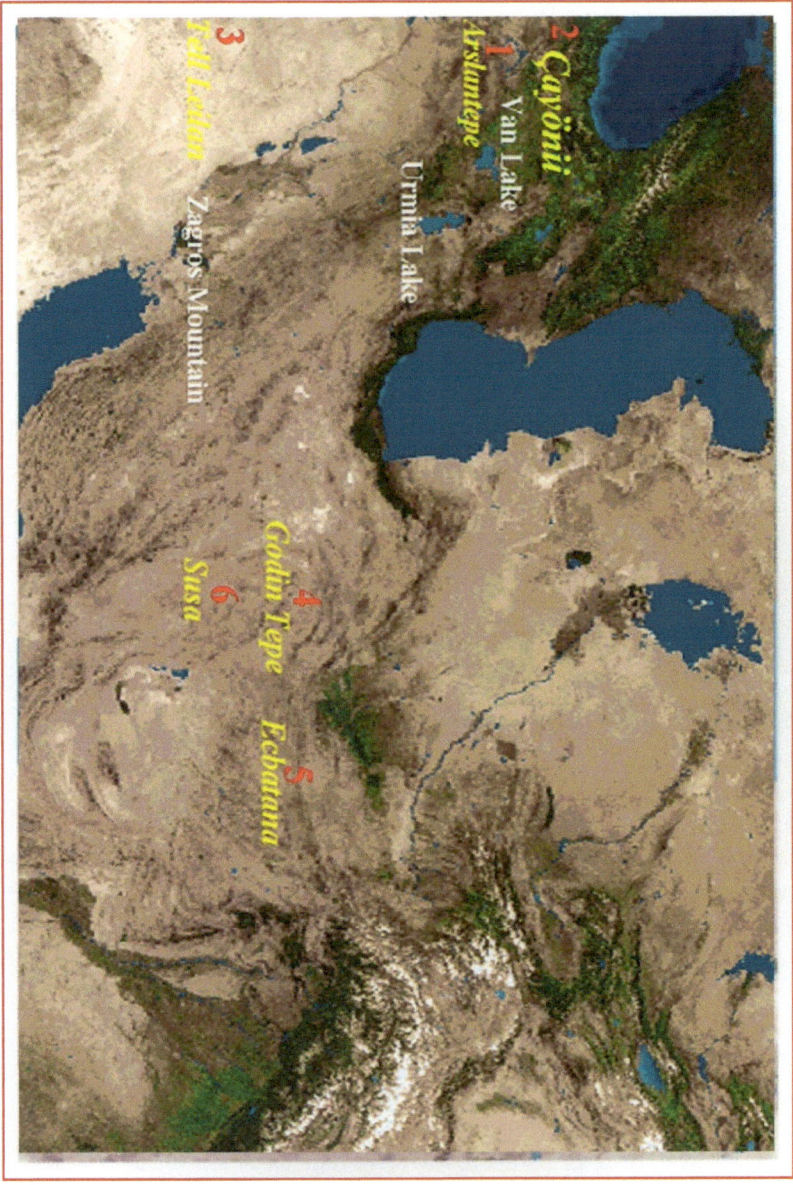

Fig. 1: Wild Euro-Asiatic grape distribution between Mediterranean and Persian Gulf

The currently cultivated vines are originated from the *Vitis vinifera sylvestris* (Mediterranean), and from the Euro-Asiatic *Vitis vinifera sativa*[42]. According to the last genetic investigations (Maxted, Ford-Loyd & Havkes 1997), they can be distinguished in a wild Mediterranean grapevine (*sylvestris*) and a wild Caucasus type, from which most of the cultivated European vines come.

The morphological diversities of *Vitis vinifera sativa* and the *Vitis vinifera sylvestris*, have been considered as steps of the evolution of the same species (Levadoux, Boubals, Rives 1962). The *Vitis vinifera sylvestris*, as a cultivated species, are begun in Greece and in Italy for an advanced anthropic action and the best environmental conditions them (Nünez & Walker 1989).

- Geographic Families

In various Mediterranean regions, the existence of populations of wild vines has been reported (Anzani et al. 1989, Levadoux 1956).

- Riparian Vegetation Families

Commonly in the Mediterranean areas the wild grapes have been observed in riparian vegetation environments, inhabited by Salix, Popolus, Alnus and Ulmus[43]. The riparian vegetation environments could have various origins, some are ancient fluvial bights, others expansion basins. What joins these environments is the presence of sweet water that allows an elevated biodiversity, constituted mainly from rich aquatic vegetation and numerous animal species.

- The Islands Family

The great islands of the Mediterranean currently have vegetation characterized by Mediterranean flora, deteriorated by the human activity. The areas in proximity of the sea are always characterized from inhospitable soils (for the salt presence). The plants have developed a strong radical apparatus, and a crawling shape to resist to the wind (*Solidago* sp., *Centaurea paniculata*, *Eryngium maritimum* and

---

[42] Rives M., 1961, Bases genetiques de la selection clonale chez la vigne, Annales d'Amelioration des Plantes, 11, 337-348.
[43] Pignatti S. 1976: Geobotanica, In: Cappelletti C., Botanica 11, 801-997, UTET, Torino.

Calystegia sp.)[44]. Generally, the grapevine is in the Mediterranean sub mountains plane, surroundings nearby marshes, lakes, and rivers (Pignatti 1976).

- Distribution of Archaeological Mediterranean Sites with Macro remains of Vitis sp.

By Archaeobotany literature we know that the *Vitis vinifera silvestris* is more ancient that one of the *Vitis vinifera sativa*. Archaeological investigations allowed the discovery in 1985 of Palaeolithic remains of grape seeds near the Conca river (Rimini)[45].

Other macro remains have been found during several diggings in the stilt houses of the Terramare[46] on some Emilia Romagna prehistoric sites.

More grape remains come from other archaeological contexts, until the Early Bronze in Tuscany[47], Lazio[48], Sardinia (Lentini 1997) and Puglia (Fig.2).

At Dimitra[49] bronze age site, and in the prehistoric Franchthi cave in Greece[50], the grapevine of *Vitis vinifera silvestris* is earlier than the grapevine of *Vitis vinifera sativa*, which appear later in the iron age.

---

[44] Lentini A. 1997: Indagini pedopalinologiche riguardanti il sito di Tharros e alcune zone circostanti, In: Acquaro E., Progetto Tharros 79-90, Agorà Edizioni, La Spezia.

[45] Nisbet R. & Rottoli M., 1997, Le analisi dei macroresti vegetali dei siti dell'età del bronzo, In: Bernabò Brea M., Cardarelli A. & Cremaschi M. (eds.), Le Terramare. La più antica civiltà padana, 469-474, Electa, Milano.

[46] Forlani L. 1988: I legni delle terramare di S. Ambrogio e di Montale. In: Cardarelli A. (ed.) Modena dalle origini all'anno Mille. Studi di archeologia e storia I: 208-209, Ed. Panini Modena; Nisbet & Rottoli 1997, 469-474.

[47] Fancelli Galletti M.L. 1974: Analisi pollinica di sedimenti sovrastanti la panchina tirreniana di Torre del Canale in Livorno, Atti Soc. Toscana Sc. Nat., Mem., ser. A, 81, 222-226, Pisa.

[48] Celant A., Follieri M., Magri D. (1996) Semi, Frutti E Carboni Nell'abitato Neolitico Di Quadrato Di Torre Spaccata (Roma). Giornale Botanico Italiano, 130 (1): 304.

[49] Renfrew J.M. 1973: Paleoethnobotany: The Prehistoric Food Plants of the Near East and Europe, Columbia Un. Press, New York - London.

[50] Hillman G.C. 1972: The Plant Remains, in: French D.H, Excavations at Can Hassan III 1969-1970, Vol. I, 180-190, Papers in Economic Prehistory, Edit by Higgs E.S., Cambridge University Press.

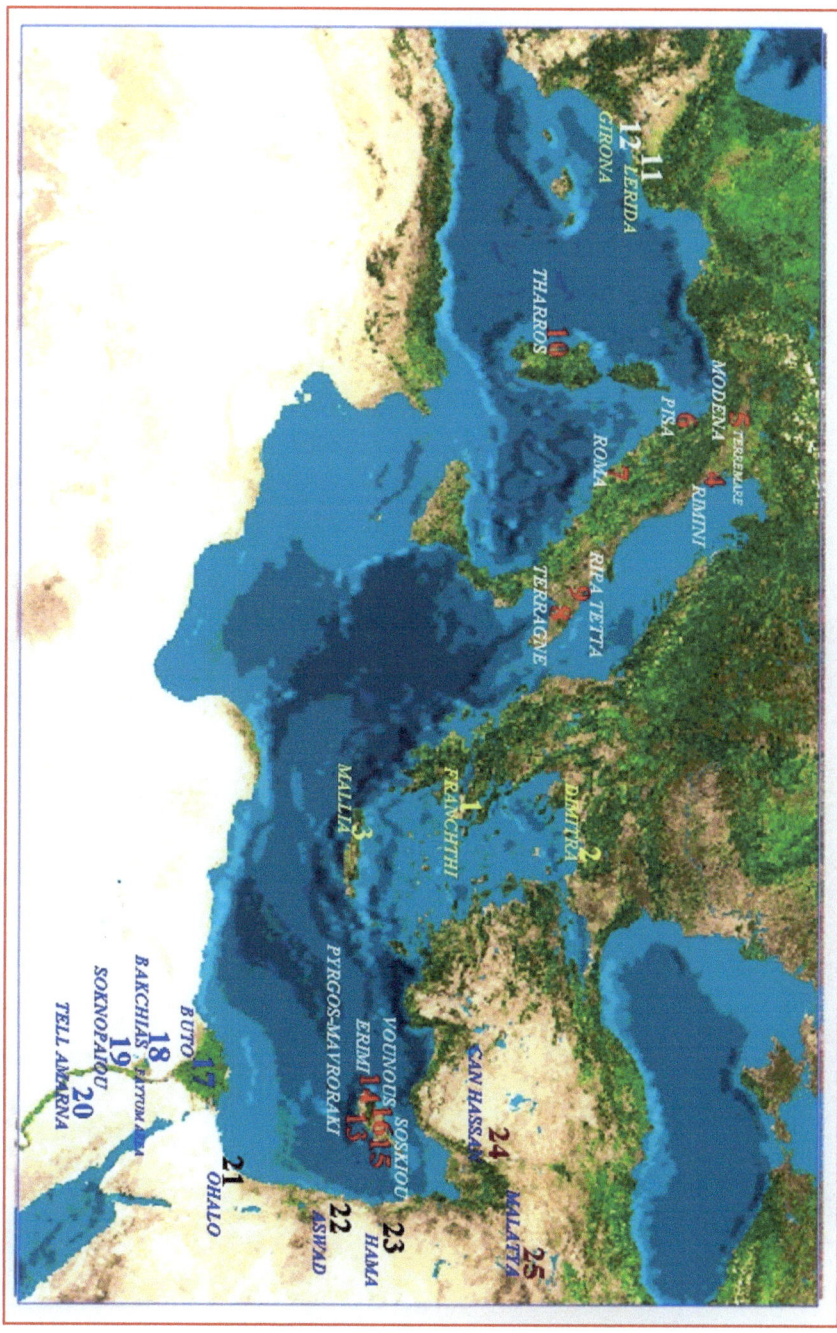

Fig. 2: Archaeological Mediterranean sites with macro remains of *Vitis sp.*

Theophrastus calls the wild grapes *Agria ampelos* (IV-III cent. BC.), as Dioscurides (1 cent. BC) that it uses the same terminology to distinguish it from the *Oenophoros ampelos*, the cultivated grape.

Virgilio in the "Eclogues" and Pliny the senior in its "Naturalis Historia" mention the Labrusca grapes as wild.

- Archaeobotanical data on the cultivation of *vitis* ssp. at Pyrgos/Mavroraki.

USPY04F8L1	Le	Wi	Th	Lt	Le/Wi	Wi/Th	Le/Th
1	3.5	5.9	2.3	1.2	0.59	2.56	1.52
2	3.2	5.11	2.15	1.05	0.62	2.37	1.48
3	3.5	6.02	2.28	1.3	0.58	2.64	1.53
4	3.3	5.55	2.19	1.18	0.59	2.53	1.5
5	3.4	5.46	2.16	1.25	0.62	2.52	1.57
6	3.3	5.5	2.21	1.19	0.60	2.48	1.49
7	3.5	6.1	2.4	1.3	0.57	2.54	1.45
8	3.5	6	2.39	1.3	0.58	2.51	1.46
9	3.3	5.52	2.2	1.18	0.59	2.50	1.50
10	3.5	6	2.39	1.3	0.58	2.51	1.46
11	3.4	5.46	2.21	1.26	0.62	2.47	1.53
12	3.5	5.96	2.35	1.3	0.58	2.53	1.48

Table n°1 - Biometric measurements of morphology roundish to heart-shaped. Labels: Le = length, Wi = width, Th = thickness, Lt = length of tip.

Archaeometry

USPY05GH9L4/5	Le	Wi	Th	Lt	Le/Wi	Wi/Th	Le/Th
1	2.8	5.23	2.16	1.1	0.83	2.42	1.29
2	2.6	5.33	2.18	1.2	0.43	2.44	1.19
3	2.4	5.18	2.2	1.38	0.46	2.35	1.09
4	2.4	5.19	2.18	1.19	0.46	2.38	1.10
5	2.2	5.14	2.13	1.22	0.42	2.41	1.03
6	2.4	5.18	2.2	1.39	0.46	2.35	1.09
7	2.8	5.25	2.18	1.24	0.53	2.4	1.28
8	2.6	5.32	2.22	1.19	0.48	2.39	1.17

Table n°2 - Biometric measurements of the morphology oval to pear-shaped, with distinctly elongated tip. Labels: Le = length, Wi = width, Th = thickness, Lt = length of tip.

USPY05L4	Le	Wi	Th	Lt	Le/Wi	Wi/Th	Le/Th
1	3.4	5.93	2.31	1.31	0.57	2.56	1.47
2	3.6	6	2.38	1.33	0.60	2.52	1.51
3	2.4	5.18	2.2	1.38	0.46	2.35	1.09
4	2.6	5.32	2.22	1.19	0.48	2.39	1.17
5	3.5	5.96	2.35	1.3	0.58	2.53	1.48
6	3.5	6	2.39	1.3	0.58	2.51	1.46
7	2.8	5.23	2.16	1.1	0.83	2.42	1.29
8	2.9	5.22	2.14	1	0.55	2.43	1.35
9	2.7	5.2	2.18	1.11	0.51	2.38	1.23
10	2.6	5.3	2	1	0.49	2.65	1.3
11	2.2	5.14	2.13	1.22	0.42	2.41	1.03

Table n°3 - Biometric measurements of morphology intermediate between that of the seeds of wild and cultivated grapes.
Labels: Le = length, Wi = width, Th = thickness, Lt = length of tip.

Our morphological characterization of the whole seeds was keyed to several distinctive ampelographic features.

We sought to distinguish the wild subspecies from the cultivated one, based on the morphological descriptions and biometric measurements reported in the literature (Stumer A. 1911, Schiemann E. 1959, Renfrew J.M. 1973, Nùñez D.G. and Walker M.J. 1989.).

USPY06L5/2	Le	Wi	Th	Lt	Le/Wi	Wi/Th	Le/Th
1	2.4	5.19	2.18	1.19	0.46	2.38	1.1
2	3.4	5.84	2.28	1.1	0.58	2.56	1.49
3	2.1	4.98	2	1	0.42	2.49	1.05
4	2.2	5.14	2.13	1.22	0.42	2.41	1.03
5	3.5	5.9	2.31	1.31	0.59	2.55	1.51
6	3.3	5.55	2.19	1.18	0.59	2.53	1.5
7	3.1	5.51	2.16	1.14	0.56	2.55	1.43
8	2	5	1.98	1.1	0.40	2.52	1.01
9	2.3	5.12	2.12	1.15	0.44	2.41	1.08
10	3.5	5.96	2.35	1.3	0.58	2.53	1.48

Table n°4 - Biometric measurements of morphology intermediate between that of the seeds of wild and cultivated grapes.
Labels: Le = length, Wi = width, Th = thickness, Lt = length of tip.

- Materials and method

Microscopic analyses aimed at identifying the morphological characteristics, biometrics, and other measurement of the various artefacts occurred to establish their origin and the technologies used to make them. The morpho-biometric study of the different archaeobotanical materials (seeds, pollens, and textile fibres), was carried out with an image analyser.

The image analysis system was composed of various technical components: a JVC C322 RGB microscope video camera mounted on a J.S. MP 3502M optical microscope and a N.135 optical stereo microscope connected to a computer with a video imaging board and a high-resolution monitor to characterise the obtained images.

A new software programme "Image Analysis and Measurement" (Findlay F. 1995) permitted either black and white or colour pictures to be acquired.

The images obtained through the optical video microscope were acquired in true colour, to avoid the false colours obtained by commercial software. Pictures were acquired as Raster (binary matrix with an x - y origin) images, which may reach a maximum size of 800 x 600 pixels. A colour threshold (Grieson P. 1986) common to all morphologies was established through operations in which areas / zones of the image (Berns R.S. 1999) under study were evidenced.

Diameters, numbers, area, radii, and orientation of several morphological characteristics were extracted automatically.

In addition, a series of mathematical equalisations, scaled enlargements and geometrical reflections made it possible to evidence distinctive structural features both in the archaeobotanical remains.

Besides, the use of the fractal dimension method (FD) is a value describing the shape-filling capacity of a rough boundary.

The concept of FD is based on the non-Euclidean system of geometry (Mandelbrot B.P., 1992) and it has been used in several research applications.

Calculating an FD for a given object is a complex procedure based upon the measurement of area, perimeter, and segments in terms of decreasing units of measurement, and requires a significant amount of data processing.

Although this is essentially a geometric measured approach it is a method that can be modified for the processing of digitally stored images. Because this factor has been applied in several studies its application to fretting particle shape description was attempted in the present study.

The system also allows the video images to be saved in B / W or RGB as TIF (Tagged Image Format) files, JPEG (Compliant), RAS (Sun Raster Images), TGA (True Vision Images), and so on, which may be opened and read by most digital image non-dedicated programs.

The morphology of seeds

The biometric size of 15 of the seeds is small; they are short, their shapes range from roundish to heart-shaped, and their tips are not prominent (Fig. 3).

The ventral part is flattish, with very slight protuberances and two deep and narrow furrows separated by a longitudinal bridge. On the dorsal part, there is an evident circular-to-oval depression of the chalaza.

These morphological features seem very much like those of wild grapes. Another group of eleven seeds has a larger biometric size; they are long and slender, from oval to pear shaped and with distinct elongated tips (Fig. 4). In the ventral part, the sculpted features are less evident and more delicate.

Fig. 3: Grape seed from SU PY05/GH9L4
Morphology roundish to heart-shaped.

The ampelographic characteristics of this group are very like the ones described in the literature for cultivating grapes. The third group's morphological features are midway between those of wild grapes and those of the apparently cultivated grapes. (Fig. 5).

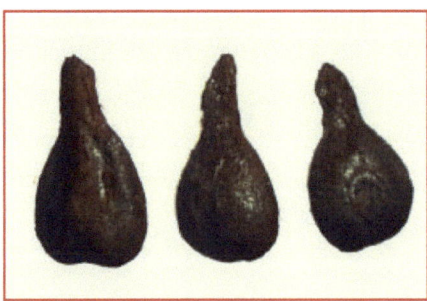

Fig. 4: Grape seeds from SU PY06L5/2
Morphology oval to pear-shaped, with distinct elongated tip.

The seeds in this group probably come from selected ecotypes (gathered in different places and in the process of being domesticated) in a context of segregation of genetic traits characteristic of an anomalous environment such as that of the islands.

The carbonization and fossilization undergone by the seeds in silt sediments (Lentini A. 2007) altered their original biometric size.

Fig. 5: Grape seeds from SU PY04F8L1 Morphology intermediate between that of seeds of wild and cultivated grapes.

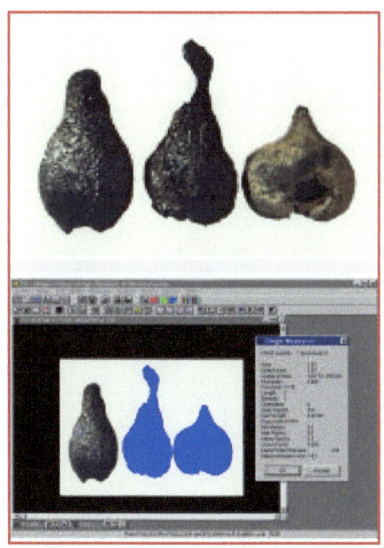

Fig. 6: SUs G9L3, G9L4 G9l7, carbonized seeds of different type of *Vitis* ssp. -- Image processing colour threshold for the biometric measurements.

Accordingly, the only dimensions we measured (using an image Analyzer- Figure 4 and Image processing 1) were the length, width and thickness of each seed and the length of the tip (Di Vora A. and Castelletti L. 1995).

We then calculated the ratios among these dimensions (Tables 1, 2, 3 and 4). The length/width index is considered a statistically significant parameter for the attribution of each seed (Castelletti L., Castiglioni E., Cottini M. and Di Vora A. 1996). A seed is thought to belong to the wild species if the index is between 0.76 and 0.83, to the cultivated species if the index is between 0.33 and 0.44, and unidentifiable if the index is between 0.54 and 0.75 (Di Vora A. and Castelletti L., 1995).

These preliminary data on the first 41 seeds are not statistically significant, but they can be taken as a preliminary indication of the distribution of the various *Vitis* species at Pyrgos (Fig.6).

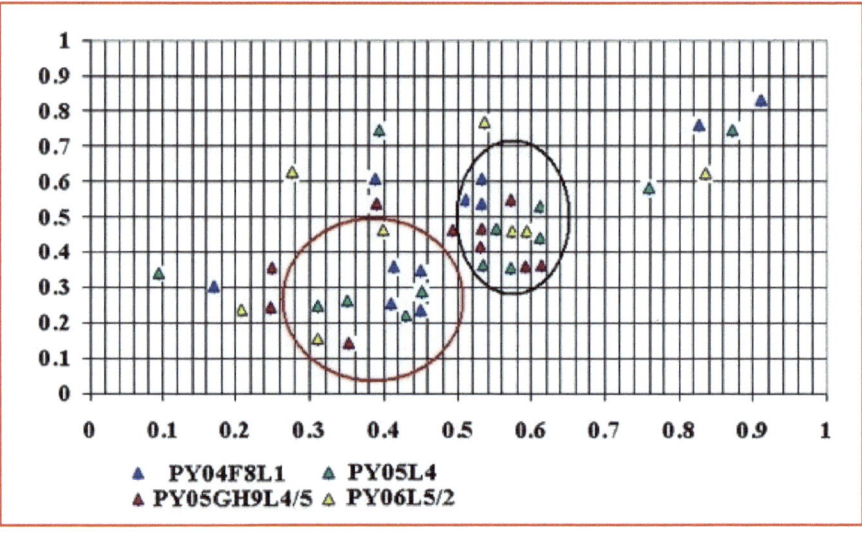

Graph 1 – Distribution of length/width measurements.

The distribution graph (Graph 1) of the length/width ratios shows a first group of 11 seeds positioned in the 0.34-0.43 range typical of cultivated grapes (Fig.7).

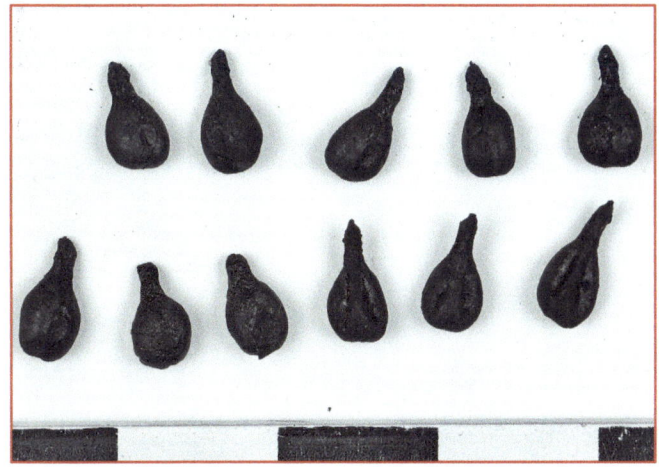

Fig.7: First group of *vitis* seeds from Pyrgos/Mavroraki typical of cultivated grapes.

A second group of 15 seeds falls in the 0.56-0.63 range, intermediate between wild and cultivated grapes and not identified with any certainty (Fig.8). The rest of the samples we examined have more homogeneous biometric traits and fall partly in the intermediate area (proto-domesticated) and partly in the area of wild species.

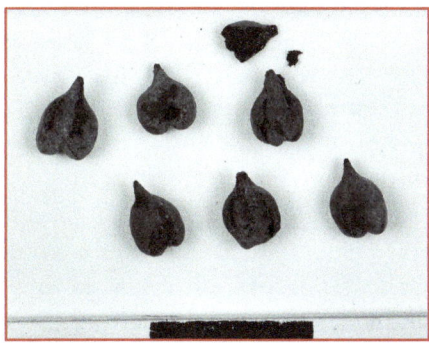

Fig.8: Second group of vitis seeds from Pyrgos/Mavroraki; intermediate range between wild and cultivated grapes.

The biotypes in the cultivated-grape range seem to ensure a good epicarp/mesocarp ratio, probably obtained by a mass based selection of multiple species (Levadoux L., 1956). The morpho-biometric variability evidenced by these studies raises a series of questions regarding biodiversity in a territory that forms part of a genetically isolated context. About the taxonomic keys used here, it should be noted that according to the *Flora Europea* (Webb D.A., 1968), the species *Vitis vinifera* L. includes the wild grapevine, *Vitis vinifera* L. ssp. *sylvestris* (C.C. GMELIN) HEGI, and the cultivated grapevine, *Vitis vinifera* ssp. *vinifera*. *Vitis sylvestris* C.C. GMELIN is used as a synonym for the wild vine and *Vitis vinifera* L. ssp. *sativa* HEGI as a synonym for the cultivated vine.

Archaeometry and Archaeology

The Smithsonian Institute (1965-1990) began in 1960, the catalogue of the official and the informatics Bibliography of the various multidisciplinary systems to characterize the organic material in ancient contexts, helping the invention of new methodologies and analytical instruments. Chemists, physics, biological and mathematical sciences, have therefore supplied to solve archaeological problems offering new possibilities.

In the last years, chromatography, spectrometry, magnetic resonance, and microscopes have been able to give advantage to archaeological investigations. The results obtained under the application of such technologies have given qualitative and quantitative measurements of ancient organic materials even from micrograms.

Many pigments, residual foods, drinks, ingredients for scents and therapeutic substances, found in special archaeological contexts (dry environment, semi deserted or saturates of humidity, where the microbial activity and the self-oxidation are reduced), and in state of medium good conservation, could have been analysed and characterized.

<u>Wine production at Pyrgos/Mavroraki and Erimi</u>

The sediments on the bottom of a vase, coming from the US Py04 G8 n°13 (Fig.9), have been extracted (elutriation) with H_2SO_4 to 20 %, for ten minutes. After, to the super floating it has been added 0,02 gr. of 0,02 gr. di ß, ß' – binaphthol (Feigl F. 1989). The obtained solution submitted to irradiation with UV lamp of 240-250 nanometres, assumed a green colour under the fluorescent rays.

Archaeometry

Fig.9: Fragment of askos from US Py04 G8 n°13: the green coloration of the solution reveals that it contains high rate of tartaric acid, typical of the wine produced in the Mediterranean area.

Fig.10: Wine jug US Py05 I 7 n. 238; analysis results

In parallel a certified synthetic sample (Ultra Scientific Italy n° 325 Organic Standards in Organic Basic solution, Oeko-Tex Standard 100 ISO 9001) has been examined with the same procedures, analytics of tartaric acid isomer present in nature, shape of L (+).

This technique (Colour Test) seems to be today one of the most efficient in the study of organic archaeological remains.

The same system has been used to analyse more residuals of some Middle Bronze Age vases coming from Pyrgos (Table n°5) with a positive result.

PYRGOS	TARTARIC ACID	RESULTS
PY02IL6 n° 3 - Residues	POSITIVE** GREEN	2
PY03J4L4 n° 4 - Residues	POSITIVE** GREEN	2
PY04F1G8 n° 2 - Residues	POSITIVE*** GREEN	3
PY04F1G8 n° 3 - Residues	POSITIVE**** GREEN	4
PY05JI7-8 - Residues	POSITIVE*** GREEN	3
PY02IL6 n° 3 - Residues	POSITIVE** GREEN	2
PY04FG8 n° 4 - Residues	POSITIVE*** GREEN	3
PY03 J4 L4 - Residues	POSITIVE** GREEN	2
PY05 JI 7-9 - Residues	POSITIVE**** GREEN	4

Table n°5 - Residual chemical analyses of the organic matter of some Middle Bronze Age vases coming from Pyrgos.

ID	TARTARIC ACID	RESULTS
ERIMI NECROPOLIS - GRAVES 115 n° 1	POSITIVE**** GREEN	4
ERIMI NECROPOLIS - GRAVES 52 n° 3	POSITIVE ** GREEN	2
ERIMI NECROPOLIS - GRAVES 105 n° 7	POSITIVE **** GREEN	4
ERIMI NECROPOLIS - GRAVES 121 n° 1	POSITIVE **** GREEN	4
ERIMI NECROPOLIS - GRAVES 118 n° 1	POSITIVE **** GREEN	4
ERIMI NECROPOLIS - GRAVES 115 n° 13	POSITIVE **** GREEN	4
ERIMI NECROPOLIS - GRAVES 97 n° 5	POSITIVE ** GREEN	2
ERIMI NECROPOLIS - GRAVES 115 n° 11	POSITIVE ** GREEN	2
ERIMI NECROPOLIS - GRAVES 115 n° 14	POSITIVE ** GREEN	2
ERIMI NECROPOLIS - GRAVES 112 n° 2	POSITIVE ** GREEN	2
ERIMI NECROPOLIS - GRAVES 92 n° 3	POSITIVE **** GREEN	4
ERIMI NECROPOLIS - GRAVES 119 n° 1	POSITIVE **** GREEN	4
ERIMI NECROPOLIS - GRAVES 115 n° 2	POSITIVE **** GREEN	4

Table 6 - Residual chemical analyses of the organic matter coming from some vases of the Erimi Necropolis.

After the setting of the methodology, other intact sediments coming from the bottom of wine amphorae from Erimi necropolis (Table 6) of a different period have been analysed as at the Limassol Archaeological Museum (Table 7) and at the Cyprus Archaeological Museum of Nicosia (Table 8).

Three different residues were extracted from Vounous, Kyrenia (drinking horn of 2000 BC), from Soskiou (3000 BC) and from Ayios Tychonas. All the exanimate Cypriote samples gave positive results regarding the tartaric acid.

I D	TARTARIC ACID	RESULTS
ERIMI 1933 - RESIDUES AMPHORA	POSITIVE * GREEN CLEAR	1
ERIMI N° 7 - RESIDUES AMPHORA	POSITIVE **** GREEN	4
ERIMI n° 6 - RESIDUES AMPHORA	POSITIVE **** GREEN	4
ERIMI n° 4 - RESIDUES AMPHORA	POSITIVE **** GREEN	4
ERIMI n° 127 EX - RESIDUES AMPHORA	POSITIVE * GREEN CLEAR	1
ERIMI n° 3 EX - RESIDUES AMPHORA	POSITIVE **** GREEN	4
ERIMI n° 9 EX - RESIDUES AMPHORA	POSITIVE **** GREEN	4
ERIMI n° 127 EX 3 - RESIDUES AMPHORA	POSITIVE * GREEN CLEAR	1
ERIMI n° 127 EX 2 - RESIDUES AMPHORA	POSITIVE **** GREEN	4
ERIMI n° 127 EX 1 - RESIDUES AMPHORA	POSITIVE **** GREEN	4
ERIMI NR-RA 2 EX - RESIDUES AMPHORA	POSITIVE **** GREEN	4
ERIMI EX 5 - RESIDUES AMPHORA	POSITIVE **** GREEN	4
ERIMI n° 140/160 - RESIDUES AMPHORA	POSITIVE **** GREEN	4
ERIMI n° 127 EX 4 - RESIDUES AMPHORA	POSITIVE * GREEN CLEAR	1

Table 7 - Residual chemical analyses of the organic matter coming from Erimi at the Limassol Archaeological Museum.

The glycolysis or fermentation of the sugars is the natural production of energy for the maintenance of life. But every product deriving from the fermentation of organic material in aerobic environment transforms itself in a short time like the wine in vinegar.

The juice of the grape ferments for the presence of natural yeast and tartaric acid, transforming own sugars in alcohol (Pisani P.L., 1991), until the alcoholic rate extinguishes the action of the yeast.

The process therefore continues transforming the wine into vinegar.

I D	TARTARIC ACID	RESULTS
AYIOS TICHONAS 2005	POSITIVE**** GREEN	4
KYRENIA (DRINKING HORN)	POSITIVE **** GREEN	4
SOUESKION (277)	POSITIVE * GREEN CLEAR	1
VOUNOS N° 61	POSITIVE **** GREEN	4

Table n° 8 - Residual chemical analyses of the organic matter coming from the vases conserved at the Archaeological Museum of Nicosia

Until the Roman period the wine making didn't know any inhibitor to arrest the process, as the Sulphur (Seltmann C. 1989) and it's probable that various systems have been experimenting to conserve the wine unaltered.

Perhaps the more used system has been the use of resin.

In the analytical investigations, conduct on various typologies of organic and inorganic materials from Pyrgos (Belgiorno M.R., Lentini A. And Scala G, 2006) and in the samples taken inside pottery probably related to the wine, have found resins of Coniferae, ssp. and *Amygdalus communis* L. probably used like inhibitors of the fermentation (Mllis J. and White R. 1989).

The archaeological sediments on the bottom of a vase, coming from Erimi, have been extracted (elutriation) with H_2SO_4 to 20 %, for ten minutes. After, the super floating 0, 02 gr. of 0, 02 gr. di ß, ß' – binaphthol was added.

The obtained solution submitted to irradiation, under a UV lamp of 240-250 nanometres, assumed a green colour under the fluorescent rays. The green coloration of the solution reveals that it contains a high rate of tartaric acid (Fig.12), typical of the wine produced in the Mediterranean area.

Fig.11: Analyses result on a fragment of jar (as example on the right) from the excavation of P. Dikaios at Erimi 1933, n°127 ex 2.

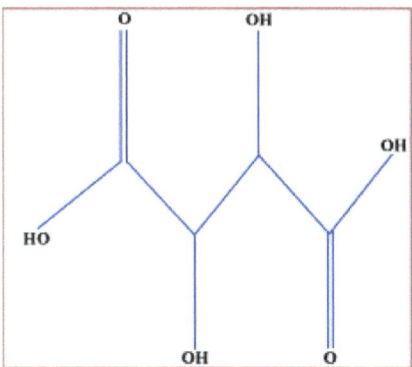

Fig. 12 - Chemical structure of tartaric acid, generally in nature, is found like Dextro-rotary stereoisomer (if illuminated with polarized light rotates towards the right). During the *fossilization*, it is transformed in a racemic acid.

The resin of the turpentine tree (*Pistacia terebinthus* L.), characterized many times (Lentini A. and Scala G. 2004) at Pyrgos - Mavroraki, during the analyses confirmed the presence of *Pistacia terebinthus* pollens in the stratigraphic section PY04 US J4, (levels -180> -230 cm, Fig. 13); composed of groups of triterpenoids compounds generally unsaturated. Such compositions are generally a group of polycyclic unsaturated, and has the function of anti-oxidants.

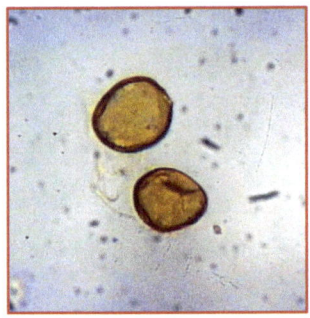

Fig. 13: Pyrgos, Stratigraphic Units PY J4, levels -180 > -230 cm, pollens of *Pistacia*.

The triterpenoids of the Anacardiaceae family (*Pistacia*) have rendered some and are all-acid, the names (oleanolic acid, masticadienonic acid, iso-masticadienonic acid) of it suggest the uses, sources and possible effects in the long term (Al-Said M.S., Ageel A.M., Parmar N.S and Tariq M. 1986).

They are constituted from a fixed unit of isoprene, characterized by five atoms of carbon, that is the base of the "mastica", the natural gum, (chew) (Pedretti M. 1997), used still today to cure the pathologies of the digesting apparatus (Marone P., Bono L., Leone E., Bona S., Carretto E. and Perversi L. 2001).

The turpentine instead is obtained under boiling the resin, taken from the *Pistacia terebinthus* L. (Turpentine of Cyprus or Chio), typical of the biome of Cyprus (Zohary M. 1973). The turpentine has been always used in the production of the resin wines (Mllis J. and White R. 1989).

The extracting process consisted in the boiling of the resin in water. Subsequently, after the cooling, it was filtered with vegetable cloth, and the accumulation of the resin emanated scent of fennel (Benigni R., Capra C. e Cattorini P.E. 1997). The essence could be used also blended with other scents.

Geobotany and biodiversity

Vitis micro-remains were found at the Middle Bronze Age site of Marki Alonia, near Nicosia (Adams R. and Simmons D. 1996), but because of the lack of detailed descriptions and biometric measurements, they cannot be compared from the taxonomic and morphological standpoint with the seeds found at Pyrgos.

These micro-remains raise a series of environmental questions regarding the geographic distribution of *Vitis* on Cyprus (biogeography), biodiversity in the natural landscape, and species imported or partially domesticated-adapted by human activities.

In this context, the oldest plant macro-remains seem to belong to the last defined probable biodiversity levels (Medail F. and Quezel P. 1997).

In effect, it is very hard to judge biodiversity in archaeological contexts, due mainly to the fact that no certified methods exist yet for classifying these Paleo-environmental structures, because the principal recognizable units represent different sectors of a highly variable anthropized environment.

Comparison between fruits and seeds of wild and cultivated grapes

Archaeobotanical, paleopalynological and sedimentological investigations plus exploration in the areas adjacent to the Pyrgos site (Lentini A. and Belgiorno M. R. 2008) have evidenced a series of environmental discontinuities that make Cyprus's natural landscape a highly varied one, thereby confirming indirectly the preliminary analytic results of the first investigations of stratigraphic sections (PY04G7 – 8) dating from between 1950 and 2000 BC.

Fig. 14: Lentini taking samples for the palynological stratigraphy.

For the purposes of an initial comparison of the archaeobotanical data, we updated a map of rainfall distribution on Cyprus (Zohary M. 1973) with rainfall and temperature data for the period from 1973 to 2007, to produce an updated view of possible microclimates on the island.

These data were collected at 25 weather stations (Fig. 18) located irregularly across the island, some concentrated in the central part (the Mesaoria plain, from Nicosia to Famagosta), others on the West coast (from Morocampos to Episkopi) and still others near the heights of the Troodos mountains (from Platania to Trimiklini), with significant absences in the North East, the North West and on the southern coast.

The weather data were processed with the aid of the Köppen formula (McKnight T.L. and Hess D. 2000).

$$I_a = \left[\frac{P_1}{T+10} + \frac{12P_2}{t} \right] : 2$$

P_1 = rainfall in mm
T = average annual temperature (°C)

P_2 = average rainfall in the driest month
t = average temperature in the driest month

Indexes <10 = arid climate
Indexes between 10 and 20 = subarid conditions
Indexes between 20 and 30 = subhumid conditions

Köppen formula (McKnight T.L. and Hess D. 2000).

The updated climate data – processed based on the contour lines obtained from cartographic elements reported in the past (Zohary M. 1973) show a distribution in eight microclimates that reflects the island's geological and altimetric features.

In fact, some areas are marked off by geographic barriers (the Troodos and Kyrenia mountains) and their characteristics of their plant populations are allopatric, while others are marked off by abiotic factors (climatic elements and soil characteristics) that operate in the same geographic area with various sympatric plant species.

On the northern side of the island, the Kyrenia mountain range b about 100 km long and rising to over 1000 meters runs parallel to the coastline and forms a sort of natural barrier between the coast and the interior (Fig.15).

The Kyrenia Mountains are the southernmost part of the Alpine-Himalayan range; they are made up mainly of Mesozoic limestone and are characterized by low precipitation and thermoclastic phenomena.

The Kyrenia rocks have low thermal conductivity values (Malikkides C. 2006), which explains why large temperature differences occur between their outer and inner parts, generating stress that causes the rocks to crumble.

Three microclimates were identified in this area (Figure 18), and are also found beyond the Mesaoria plain.

-The most extensive one, referable to the Kyrenia weather station (Fig. 18, no. 2), includes the mountainous area that slopes down to the sea, and is characterized by soils consisting for the most part of Dolomitic limestone with a high degree of salinity.

Fig. 15: Kyrenia mountain range about 100 km long and rising to over 1000 meters runs parallel to the coastline and forms a sort of natural barrier between the coast and the interior.

Here the most representative biome is made up of *Juniperus phoenicea* (the Syrian element) and various seasonal halophytes, while *Pinus brutia* is present in the medium-to high altitudes.

-The second microclimate, referable to the Haleuga station (Fig. 18, no. 3), is divided into three small areas, distant from each other, at the highest altitudes in the Kyrenia's; here the ground is rocky (sub-acid, limestone) and there is no significant stable vegetation.

-The third microclimate characterizes a large area with allopatric features, the northwest-northeast area between Kormakiti and the tip of Cape Andreas. Only one weather station monitors it at Vahlia (Fig. 18, no. 6). It is separated from the rest of the same distribution range from the Mesaoria plain to the south (Fig. 3) and southeast; by the desert area monitored by the Morphou station (Fig. 18, no. 7).

To the northwest and, in the southern part of the island and to the southwest, it is separated by the lower reaches of the Troodos Mountains, which slope down to the sea.

Almost all the weather stations covering this microclimate are located along the coasts: at Ktima, Paphos, Morocampos, Patria tou Romiou and Episkopi in the southwest (Fig. 18, nos. 20-24), near Limassol in the south (Fig. 18, no. 25), and at Larnaca in the South East (Fig. 18, no. 14).

The soils in these areas have a medium texture; in the more internal areas they have a high carbonate content and are subject to frequent leaching phenomena, while in the areas adjacent to the coastline high percentages of sodium and potassium characterize them.

The native vegetation consists of Irano-Turanic species (*Cupressus sempervirens, Pinus halepensis* and *Cedrus* ssp.) and Mediterranean species (*Prunus, Pistacia, Olea europea* L., *Quercus, Ceratonia, Myrtus* and *Laurus*) variously distributed across the territory according to local variables (Meikle R. D. 1977, 1985). Growing near the short streams are *Populus, Salix, Miriophyllum* ssp. and other aquatic grasses.

-The fourth microclimate, with less than 300 mm of rainfall per year, according to the data reported by the Morphou weather station (Fig. 18, no. 7), is the island's only desertified area. As the soil is made up of calcareous sands with a high degree of salinity, it is subject to evapotranspiration phenomena. The vegetation that grows here during short periods of the year consists of halophytes (Chenopodiaceae, Amaranthaceae and *Salsola* ssp.).

-The fifth microclimate is one of the islands largest; it includes the Mesaoria plain, which has the highest concentration of weather stations, at Kokkini Trimithia, Nicosia, Athalassa, Prastio and Famagosta (Fig. 18, nos. 8-12). This territory, nearly all irrigated and farmed, is the one that has been most intensely affected by human activities over the course of history.

It has a record of deforestation (Gomex Campo C. 1985), wildfires and farming methods that have eroded and impoverished the soil, leading to the formation of Garrigues associated with anthropocore species, mainly *Quercus coccifera, Olea europea* L., *Olea europea* L. var. *sylvestris* (wild olive), *Ceratonia* ssp. (carob), Graminaceae, *Genista* ssp., *Calycotome* ssp., Chenopodiaceae-Amaranthaceae, Asteraceae, Labiatae and Compositae.

The garrigue is the next to last stage in the regression of Mediterranean phytoclimatic associations, after the Oleo-Ceratonion xerophile scrub and before the steppe. Its widespread presence in a Mediterranean region can be taken as an indicator of desertification.

Also, present in this microclimate are some wetlands that are considered marginal, including streams and lakes near Famagosta. Associations of halophytes characterized them (*Juncus* ssp., *Spartina* ssp., *Salicornia fruticosa* and *Arthrocnemum fruticosum*). In this area, there is a disjunction toward the southeast, near the border between Kiti and Larnaca. In the spring, the vegetation here consists mainly of *Ulva* ssp., *Enteromorpha* ssp. and *Chaetomorpha* ssp.

-The other three microclimates are in the Troodos mountains, at altitudes between 1600 and 1900 meters, and on up to the highest peak of Mt. Olympus (1952 meters) monitored by weather stations of Platania, Prodhromos, Stravos, Trimiklini and Lania villages (Fig.16).

The limestone foothills are subject to Karst phenomena, with the formation of dolinas and sinkholes. Sandstone and conglomerates are also present in some parts of these areas.

Fig. 16: *Populus, Alnus* and *Salix* along the streams.

The vegetation on these lower slopes consists of evergreens (*Cupressus sempervirens* and *Juniperus phoenicea*), semideciduous trees

(*Quercus coccifera* and *Quercus infectoria*) and *Arbutus andrachne*. Along the streams that flow down from the higher altitudes are large woods made up of *Populus, Salix* and *Alnus*.

At the lowest altitudes, near the sea, the beds of these streams usually remain dry during the spring and summer. At altitudes of around 900-1000 meters, *Vitis vinifera* L ssp. *sativa* HEGI is cultivated on man-made terraces with the "little tree" method (Fig.17). The vines, each one set in a small hollow that protects the grapes from the hot winds, and pruned to a height of 30-40 centimetres. A few "branches" grow on each "tree," each branch is left with one or more shoots, each shoot with one or two buds.

Fig. 17: Cultivation of *Vitis vinifera* L. ssp. *sativa* HEGI by the "little tree" method at an altitude of 900 - 1000 meters (Troodos mountains).

The territories lying above 1000 meters in the Troodos Mountains are made up of igneous and pillow-lava formations originated by molten lava that poured into the sea as the Eurasiatic plate drifted away from the Arabian plate.

The biome most representative of these areas is the vast pine woods, made up mainly of *Pinus brutia* and the endemic species *Cedrus brevifolia*, associated with *Quercus alnifolia,* likewise an endemic species. At the higher altitudes near Mt. Olympus are *Pinus Palladian* woods, with *Juniperus foetidissima* present in the glades.

The pine forest was Cyprus's original biome, and in the past, it's probably covered a large part of the island (Quezel P. 1979). At present this biome occupies some residual areas near Paphos (at sea level), as well as the areas at the highest altitudes. In the past, human activities and climate changes seemed to have drastically impoverished the original biome (Lentini and Belgiorno 2008).

Overall, the vegetation on Cyprus, as in other Mediterranean areas, is the result of glacial movements in the Quaternary era, when species native to continental Europe retreated to territories on the Mediterranean Sea. Besides furthering the preservation of these northern species, the Mediterranean areas became the evolutionary environments of individual species (Strasburger E., Noll F., and Schenck H. 1990). Cyprus was one of the Mediterranean islands whose orographic features encouraged the phylogenetic evolution of many species, and today it is especially rich in endemic species (Pantelas V., Papachristophorou T., and Christodoulou P. 1993).

Endemism is widespread on many Mediterranean islands (Sardinia, Corsica, Sicily, Malta, Cyprus, Crete, Zante), where conditions are favourable for speciation, due to the presence of geographic and abiotic barriers that hinder dispersion of the original genetic makeup.

They are especially numerous on the islands that have been separated longest from the mainland. The great diversity of habitats and microclimates on Cyprus makes for an abundance of native species.

Their number is estimated at 179 (Pantelas V. et alii. 1993), and their distribution ranges from the Troodos Mountains (87) to the Kyrenia

(57) and the Akamas peninsula (35). Systematic botanists consider some of them, such as the Cyprus cedar *(Cedrus brevifolia)* and the Cyprus oak *(Quercus alnifolia)* to be living fossils (Pantelas V. et alii., 1993). The aromatic species *Nepeta troodi, Teucrium cyprium, Teucrium micropodioides, Thymus integer, Salvia willeana* and *Origanum cordifolium* are thought to be among the major evolutionary lines of the officinal species that are most widespread and best known in the Mediterranean region.

Very rare bulb species such as *Cyclamen cyprium, Tulipa cypria, Crocus cyprius, Crocus veneris, Chionodoxa lochiae* and *Gagea juliae* have sometimes been used as officinal species (IUCN - Centres of Plant Diversity, 1994), and on some occasions in the past were pictured on pottery, mosaics, and other objects of high artistic value (Codex Julianae Aniciae). Cyprus's location on the south-easterly boundary between the Mediterranean region, the Pontic region (the Irano-Turanic element) and the Near East (the Syriac and Nubo-Sindic elements) (Zohary D. 1996) does not seem to have effectively influenced the most important endemic species; they were probably preserved by the island's microclimates and edaphic conditions.

Our analysis of the seeds of the various species of *Vitis* found at Pyrgos, taking together with the results of the sedimentological and paleopalynological tests, indicates that optimal conditions existed for the cultivation of *Vitis* at low altitudes (100 – 200 m) near the sea (4 km away), in an environment very different from the one in which *Vitis vinifera* L. ssp. *sativa* HEGI is cultivated today on the slopes of the Troodos mountains, at much higher altitudes (900-1100 meters).

The preliminary results obtained at Pyrgos suggest that the local climate was cool and moist, as has been found at other southern Mediterranean sites dating from 1900-2000 B.C. (Palmieri A. M. 1980; Belluomini G., Esu D., Mandra L. and Matteucci R. 1980; Bar-Yosef O. 1990; Lentini A. and Palmieri A. M. 1993; Palmieri A. M. and Lentini A. 1994; Rögl F. 1999).

In those environmental conditions, when the climate was cool and moist, the vegetation now found at medium and high altitudes likely grew at lower altitudes closer to the sea. Later on, due partly to the evolution of the climate and the environment in all the Mediterranean territories toward sub-arid periods (Barbero M. and Quezel P. 1979), and partly to increasingly intense human activities, the most representative biocenoses gradually moved to higher altitudes, where the environmental conditions were still cool and moist.

Conclusions

The biodiversity of several environments from which the greatest sources of documentation on the origin and the spread of the *Vitis vinifera sylvestris* and *Vitis vinifera sativa* come, presents a series of acclimatize and chronological problems.

The terms of comparison, between the countries of the Mediterranean and the TransCaucasus, possess many contrasts for the number and the quality of the produced documentation (typology of the manufactory ones, palaeontology, dating, survey, geomorphology, sedimentology, Archaeobotany, Archaeometry, conservation and restoration).

In fact, the Mediterranean sites, representing various periods and environments, with punctual attestations and chronology, while, the Trans-Caucasus area documentation appears fragmented as for the processing as for the chronology. It makes exception the important job of Vavilov and the immense archaeological and Archaeometry documentation of the Turks sites of Malatya (29), Arslantepe, Can Hassan (15) and Cayonu Tepesi (12).

The comparison between the preliminary analytical results of Pyrgos and Erimi and the evidences coming from the analyses of Godin Tepè in Iran (Weiss H. and T. Cuyler Young, Jr. 1975 - Biers W. R. and McGovern P. 1990 - Badler V. 1991) is in Archaeometry interest. In fact, in both cases, the analytic procedures employed substantially agree, even if in the case of Godin Tepe the analysed material has been characterized also with spectroscopy **FT-IT/ATR** (Biers W. R. and Mc Govern P. 1990).

However, it should be considered the fact that the fragments of Godin Tepè pottery come from the same jar (dated between the 3100

- 2900 BC), while the organic residuals from Cyprus come from 41 different objects found in four sites.

Of these, 16 come from Erimi, Chalcolithic jars (half of the IV millennium BC, Museum of Limassol), 13 from Erimi Necropolis, 9 from Pyrgos-Mavroraki (beginning II millennium BC, Museum of Limassol), 1 from Vounous, Kyrenia (drinking horn of 2000 BC, Cyprus Museum) and 1 from Souskiou (3000 BC, Cyprus Museum Nicosia).

As under the statistical aspect, like under the qualitative aspect the Cypriote tests seem more concrete and they refer to a large chronological arch supported by a meaningful evolution of the pottery destined to the wine.

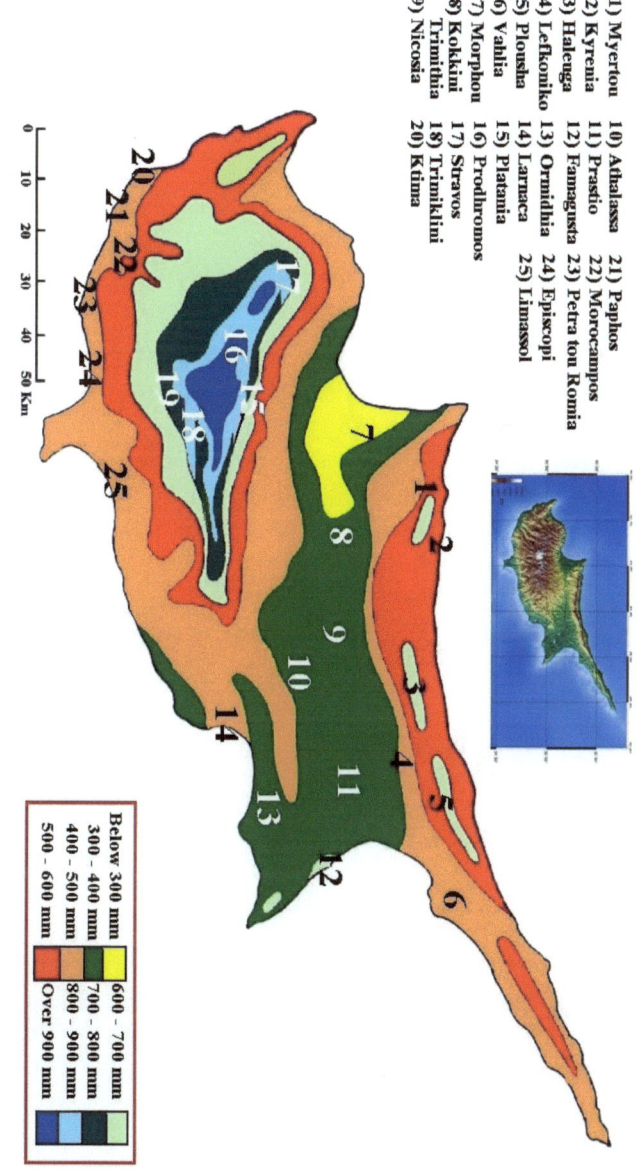

Fig. 18: Rain distribution in Cyprus.

REFERENCES

-Adams R. & Simmons D. 1996: Archaeobotanical remains, In: Frankel D. and Webb J.M., *MARKI ALONIA, An Early and Bronze Age Town in Cyprus*, Förlag P.A., Jonsered.

-Al-Said M.S., Ageel A.M., Parmar N.S. and Tariq M. 1986: Evaluation of mastic, a crude drug obtained from *Pistacia lentiscus* for gastric and duodenal anti-ulcer activity, in *Journal of Ethnopharmacol*, 15, 271-278.

-Anzani R., Failla O., Scienza A., Campostrini F. 1990: Wild grapevine (Vitis vinifera var. silvestris) in Italy: distribution, characteristics, and germplasm presentation. *1989 Report. Vitis. Special Issue*: 97-112.

-Badler V. 1991: Travels with "Jarley": a 4th millennium B.C. wine jar from Godin Tepe, *Archaeological Newsletters*, Royal Ontario Museum, 2[a], Vol.44,1-4.

-Barbero M. & Quezel P. 1979: Contribution á l'étude des groupements forestiers de Chypre, *Documents phytosociologiques 4*, Lilie.

-Bar-Yosef O. 1990: The last glacial maximum in the Mediterranean Levant, In: Soffer O. and Gamble G., *The World at 18,000 BP*, Unwin Hyman, London.

-Belgiorno M.R., Lentini A. and G. Scala 2006: Sostanze terapeutiche dal sito preistorico di Pyrgos Mavroraki (Cipro) - indagini tossicologiche preliminari, *Atti del III Congresso Nazionale di Archeometria*, C. D'Amico (ed.), IV, 757-767, Pàtron Editore, Bologna.

-Belluomini G., Esu D., Manfra L. and Matteucci R. 1980: Gasteropodi dulcicoli e terrestri nell'isola di Dahlak Kebir - testimonianze di una fase umida Olocenia nell'isola Dahlak, Mar Rosso, *Boll. Malacologico*, 16, 369-390.

-Benigni R., Capra C. and Cattorini P.E. 1997: *Piante Medicinali Chimica Farmacologia e Terapia*, vol. I, Ed. Inverni e Della Beffa, Milano.

-Berns R.S. 1999: Challenges for Color Science in Multimedia Imaging

Systems, In Mac Donald L. and Luo R., (Eds), *Colour Imaging: Vision and Technology*, John Wiley and Sons, England, 99-127.

-Biers W. R. and McGovern P. 1990: Organic Contents of Ancient Vessels: Materials Analysis and Archaeological Investigation, *MASCA Research Papers in Science and Archaeology*, Vol. 7, Philadelphia.

-Castelletti L., Castiglioni E., Cottini M. e Di Vora A. 1996: Analisi morfometrica dei vinaccioli di vite (Vitis vinifera L.) provenienti da scavi archeologici, in, *XIII International Congress of Prehistoric and Protohistoric Sciences, Forlì Italia*, 8/14 September 1996, Colloquia 3, *Palaeoecology*, 11-24.

-Celant A., Follieri M., Magri D. 1996: Semi, Frutti e Carboni Nell'abitato Neolitico Di Quadrato Di Torre Spaccata (Roma). *Giornale Botanico Italiano*, 130 (1): 304.

-Di Vora & Castelletti L. 1995: Indagine preliminare sull'archeologia della vite (*Vitis vinifera* L.) in base ai caratteri diagnostici del vinacciolo, *Rivista Archeologica dell'Antica provincia e Diocesi di Como*, 176, 333-358.

-Fancelli Galletti M.L. 1974: Analisi pollinica di sedimenti sovrastanti la panchina tirreniana di Torre del Canale in Livorno, *Atti Soc. Toscana Sc. Nat., Mem., ser. A*, 81, 222-226, Pisa.

-Feigl F. 1989: *Spot Test in Organic Analysis, Seventh Completely Revised Edition*, Elseveir, Amsterdam.

-Findlay F. 1995: *Image Analysis and Measurement*, Foster Findlay Associates Ltd, London. Gomez Campo C., 1985. *Plant Conservation in the Mediterranean Ecosystems*, Ed. Geobotanica 7, Junk Publishers, Dordrecht.

-Forlani L. 1988: I legni delle Terramare di S. Ambrogio e di Montale, in: Cardarelli A. (ed.) *Modena dalle origini all' anno Mille. Studi di archeologia e storia*, I: 208-209, Edizioni Panini, Modena.

-Grieson P. 1986: *The Color Cauldron*, Publishing Company, London.

-Hillman G.C. 1972: The Plant Remains, in: French D.H, -*Excavations at Can Hassan III 1969-1970,* Vol. I, 180-190, Papers in Economic Prehistory, Edit by Higgs E.S., Cambridge University Press.

-IUCN, Centres of Plant Diversity 1994: *A guide and strategy for their conservation*, vol. 3, IUCN Publication Service Unit, Cambridge.

-Lentini A. & Palmieri A.M. 1993: Test sedimentologico nel sito di Tharros, *Rivista Studi Fenici*, XXI, 183-190, Istituti Editoriali e Poligrafici Internazionali, Pisa – Roma.

-Lentini A. and Scala G. 2004: Fragrant substances and therapeutic compounds, in: Belgiorno M.R. *Pyrgos Mavroraki, Advanced Technology in Bronze Age Cyprus* I, 45-47, CNR Bureau President's, Nicosia.

-Lentini A. 2005: Archaeobotany brewing and winemaking in Mediterranean basin and TransCaucasus area, in: Flourentzos P., Belgiorno M.R. and Lentini A., *Cyprus in the Prehistory of Wine*, MAE Ambasciata d'Italia a Nicosia, 11-16.

-Lentini A. & Belgiorno M.R. 2008: Archaebotanical investigations at Pyrgos-Mavroraki (Cyprus), preliminary results. *IV International Cyprological Congress*, Nicosia – Cyprus.

-Levadoux L. 1956: 'Les populations sauvages et cultivées de *Vitis vinifera* L.', *Annales de l'"Amelioration des Plantes*, 10, 40-71.

-Levadoux L, Boubals D. & Rives M. 1962: Le genre Vitis et ses especes, *Ann. Amelior.* Pl. 12 19-44.

-Lisitsina G.N. & Walker M.J. 1989: The Caucasus: A Centre of Ancient Farm in Eurasia. In: *Plants and Ancient Man, in Palaeoethnobotany,* (eds.) Van Zeist W. & Casparie M.A., 285-292, A.A. Balkema, Amsterdam - Boston.

-Malikkides C. 2006: Calculation methods for critical loads of acidity and nutrient nitrogen and for dynamic modelling, *Bulletin of Ministry of Labour and Social Insurance*, 1- 6 Nicosia.

Mandelbrot B.P. 1992: *The Fractal Geometry of Nature*, Freeman W.H., San Francisco.

-Marone P., Bono L., Leone E., Bona S., Carretto E. and Perversi L. 2001: Bactericidal activity of *Pistacia lentiscus* mastic gum against Helicobacter pylori, *Journal of Chemother*, 13(6), 611-4.

-McKnight T L. and Hess D. 2000: Climate Zones and Types: The Köppen System, Physical Geography: A Landscape Appreciation, Upper Saddle River, *NJ*: Prentice Hall, 200-1.

-Maxted N., Ford-Loyd B.V. & Havkes J.G. 1997: Plant Genetic Conservation, Champman & Hall, London.

-Medail, F. and Quezel P. 1997: Hotspots Analysis for Conservation of Plant Biodiversity in the Mediterranean Basin, *Ann. Missouri Garden*, 84.

-Meikle R.D. 1977, 1985: *Flora of Cyprus*, The Bentham Moxon Trust, Royal Botanical Gardens, Kew, UK.

-Miles J. & White R. 1989: The identity of the resin from the late Bronze Age Shipwreck at Ulu Burun (Kas). *In Archaeometry*, 31, 37-44.

-Nisbet R. & Rottoli M. 1997: Le analisi dei macroresti vegetali dei siti dell'età del bronzo, in: Bemabò Brea M., Cardarelli A. & Cremaschi M. (eds.), *Le Terramare. La più antica civiltà padana*, 469-474, Electa, Milano.

-Nùñez D.G. and Walker M.J. 1989: A rewiev of paleobotanical finding of early Vitis in the Mediterranean and of the origin of cultivated grape-vines with special reference to new pointers to Prehistoric exploitation in the Western Mediterranean, *Rewiev of Palaeobotany and Palynology*, 61, 205-237.

-Palmieri A.M.1980: Studio sedimentologico del saggio profondo di Coppa Nevigata (Gargano), *Quaternaria*, XXII, 301-313.

-Palmieri A.M. e Lentini A. 1994: Indagini paleopalinologiche e fisico chimiche nel quadrante meridionale della sponda ovest dello stagno di

Cabras, *Rivista Studi Fenici*, XXII, 2, 195-200, Istituti Editoriali e Poligrafici Internazionali, Pisa - Roma.

-Pantelas V., Papachristophorou T. and Christodoulou, P. 1993: *Cyprus Flora in Colour: The Endemics*, Nicosia, Cyprus.

-Pedretti M. 1997: *Chimica e Farmacologia delle Piante Medicinali*, Edizioni Studio, Milano.

-Pignatti S. 1976: Geobotanica, In: Cappelletti C., *Botanica 11*, 801-997, UTET, Torino.

-Pisani P.L. 1991: Historical aspects of the vine and wine in Italy, *Alcologia*, A3, 1, 21-29.

-Renfrew J.M. 1973: *Palaeoethnobotany: The Prehistoric Food Plants of the Near East and Europe*, Columbia University Press, New York - London.

-Quezel P. 1979: Les écosystemes forestiers crétois et chypriotes, *Chroniques intern, RFF*, 31.

-Rögl F. 1999: *Oligocene and Miocene Palaeogeography and Stratigraphy of the CircumMediterranean Region*, (eds.) Whybrow P. J. and Hill A., vol. I, 485-500, Yale University Press, New Haven

-Schiemann E. 1953: Vitis in Neolithicum der Mark Bradenburg, *Der Zuchter*, vol. 23, 318-327.

-Seltmann C. 1989: Wine in the ancient word, in: *Plants and Ancient Man, Studies in Palaeoethnobotany*, (eds.) Van Zeist W. and Casparie M.A., 200-230, A.A. Balkema, Amsterdam - Boston.

-Smithsonian Institute: Archives 1965-1990: TSA, Washington.
-Strasburger E., Noll F. e Schenck H. 1990: *Sistematica e geobotanica*, vol. 2, 31° Edizione, Delfino Editore, Roma.

-Stumer A. 1911: Zur Urgeschichte der Rebe und des Weinbaues', In: Wien, *Mitteilungen der Anthropologischen Gesellschaft*, vol. 41, 283-296.

-Unwin T. 1991: *Wine and the Vine: An Historical Geography of Viticulture and the Wine Trade*, Books News, Portland.

-Vavilov N. L. 1950: The origin, variation, immunity and breeding of cultivated plants, Trsld. by Starr K Chester. *Chronica Botanicae*, 13, XVII, 364.

Walbot W. & Cullis C.A. 1983: The plasticity of the plant genome. Is it a requirement for success? In, *Plant Molecular Biology Report* 1, 3-14.

Webb D.A. 1968: "Vitaceae", In: Tutin T.G. et al., *Flora Europea*, vol. 2, Cambridge,.246-247. Weiss H. and T. Cuyler Young, Jr., 1975. *The Merchants of Susa, Godin V and plateau lowland relations in the late fourth millennium B.C.*, Offprint: Iran. vol. 13.

-Zohary M. 1973: *Geobotanical Foundation of the Middle East*, Vol.2, Fischer Verlag, Stuttgart, Swets and Zeitlinger, Amsterdam.

-Zohary D. 1996: The Domestication of the Grapevine *Vitis Vinifera* L. in the Near East, In: McGovern P.E. et *alii*. (eds.), *The Origins and Ancient History of Wine*, Gordon and Breach Publishes, Amsterdam, 23-30.

-Zohary D. & Hoff M. 2000: Domestication of Plants in the Old Wold: The Origin and Spread of Cultivated Plants in West Asia, Europe and the Nile Valley, Oxford, University Press.

PERSONAL NOTES

www.ingramcontent.com/pod-product-compliance
Lightning Source LLC
Chambersburg PA
CBHW042326150426
43193CB00001B/4